ROUTLEDGE LIBRARY EDITIONS: LIBRARY AND INFORMATION SCIENCE

Volume 36

EXPERIENCES OF LIBRARY NETWORK ADMINISTRATORS

EXPERIENCES OF LIBRARY NETWORK ADMINISTRATORS

Papers Based on the Symposium "From Our Past: Toward 2000"

Edited by
WILSON LUQUIRE

LONDON AND NEW YORK

First published in 1985 by The Haworth Press, Inc.

This edition first published in 2020
by Routledge
2 Park Square, Milton Park, Abingdon, Oxon OX14 4RN

and by Routledge
52 Vanderbilt Avenue, New York, NY 10017

Routledge is an imprint of the Taylor & Francis Group, an informa business

© 1985 The Haworth Press, Inc.

All rights reserved. No part of this book may be reprinted or reproduced or utilised in any form or by any electronic, mechanical, or other means, now known or hereafter invented, including photocopying and recording, or in any information storage or retrieval system, without permission in writing from the publishers.

Trademark notice: Product or corporate names may be trademarks or registered trademarks, and are used only for identification and explanation without intent to infringe.

British Library Cataloguing in Publication Data
A catalogue record for this book is available from the British Library

ISBN: 978-0-367-34616-4 (Set)
ISBN: 978-0-429-34352-0 (Set) (ebk)
ISBN: 978-0-367-40366-9 (Volume 36) (hbk)
ISBN: 978-0-367-40369-0 (Volume 36) (pbk)
ISBN: 978-0-429-35571-4 (Volume 36) (ebk)

Publisher's Note
The publisher has gone to great lengths to ensure the quality of this reprint but points out that some imperfections in the original copies may be apparent.

Disclaimer
The publisher has made every effort to trace copyright holders and would welcome correspondence from those they have been unable to trace.

Experiences of Library Network Administrators

Papers Based on the Symposium
"From Our Past: Toward 2000"

Wilson Luquire
Editor

The Haworth Press
New York

Experiences of Library Network Administrators has also been published as *Resource Sharing and Information Networks,* Volume 2, Numbers 1/2, Fall/Winter 1984.

Copyright © 1985 by The Haworth Press, Inc. All rights reserved. No part of this book may be reproduced or utilized in any form or by any means, electronic or mechanical including photocopying, microfilm, and recording, or by any information storage and retrieval system without permission in writing from the publisher. Printed in the United States of America.

The Haworth Press, Inc., 28 East 22 Street, New York, NY 10010

Library of Congress Cataloging in Publication Data
Main entry under title:

Experiences of library network administrators.

    Also published as Resource sharing & information networks, v. 2, no. 1/2, fall/winter 1984.
    Includes bibliographical references.
    1. Library information networks—United States—Administration—Congresses. I. Luquire, Wilson. II. Resource sharing & information networks.
Z674.8.E96 1984   021.6'5   84-22428
ISBN 0-86656-388-1

Experiences of Library Network Administrators

Resource Sharing and Information Networks
Volume 2, Numbers 1/2

CONTENTS

FROM THE EDITOR	1
Bridget L. Lamont, *Director, The Illinois State Library, Springfield, Illinois*	3
Welcome	5
The Honorable Wayne Anderson, Deputy Secretary of State, Chicago, Illinois	
MORNING SESSION	11
Introductory Remarks by Bridget Lamont	
The AMIGOS Experience: Development of a Successful Network	13
James H. Kennedy, Western Region Marketing Manager, OCLC, Inc., Dublin, Ohio	
Governance	14
Staff	17
Products/Services	19
Member Libraries	23
Summary	23

**Library Networks Circa 1984 or One Blind Person
 Touching the Elephant**   27
> *Alice E. Wilcox, Reference Division,
> University of Minnesota Libraries,
> Minneapolis, Minnesota*

Environment Conducive to Networking	30
MINITEX Focus and Structure	32
Observations Regarding the Impact of Networking on the Library Community	34
Lost Opportunities	36
Then There Are the "Confusing Cs"	38
Conclusion	40

The CLASS Experience   41
> *J. Michael Bruer, Director of Marketing,
> Carlyle Systems, Inc., Berkeley,
> California*

AFTERNOON SESSION

Experience and Expectation   65
> *Frederick G. Kilgour, Founder Trustee,
> OCLC, Inc., Dublin, Ohio*

Introduction	66
OCLC—Retrospection	67
Expectation	73
Summary	75

**The National Commission on Libraries and Information
 Sciences: Past Accomplishments—Future Prospects**   77
> *Alphonse F. Trezza, Associate Professor,
> School of Library and Information
> Studies, The Florida State University,
> Tallahassee, Florida*

Panel Discussion   95

FROM THE EDITOR

This issue is dedicated to the proceedings of the April 16, 1984 symposium "From Our Past: Toward 2000" held in Chicago, Illinois. The speakers represented state, regional, and national networks, and the National Commission on Libraries and Information Science.

The introductions and panel discussion are an exact recap, inasmuch as possible, of the day's activities in an attempt to have you relive the symposium as it occurred on April 16th. Our speakers were asked to prepare manuscripts of their keynote addresses for publication.

The speakers' remarks were directed toward "From Our Past: Toward 2000" in relation to their specific experiences with the state, regional, or national network in which they were/are affiliated.

Wilson Luquire
Editor

Bridget L. Lamont

Director, The Illinois State Library
Springfield, Illinois

Good morning, my name is Bridget Lamont. I'm the Director of the Illinois State Library and I have the honor of coordinating the speaking efforts throughout the program today. Although this conference has many national implications, it does occur in Illinois and those of us in Illinois know that a lot of library activity occurs because of our Secretary of State and State Librarian's activities and interest in Illinois libraries. The Secretary of State Jim Edgar is unable to be with us this morning to give us formal welcome to Illinois and Chicago. However, the Deputy Secretary of State, Wayne Anderson, will offer a few remarks. Wayne.

BRIDGET L. LAMONT: "Good morning, my name is Bridget Lamont. I'm the Director of the Illinois State Library and I have the honor of coordinating the speaking efforts throughout the program today."

Welcome

The Honorable Wayne Anderson

Deputy Secretary of State
Chicago, Illinois

Somehow, on a Monday morning on a drizzly day in Chicago I would think you'd prefer to be greeted by Bridget rather than me. It's really a pleasure for me to be here today, particularly on behalf of Secretary of State Jim Edgar. I don't get to go to as many library oriented functions as I'd like to go to, because as those of you from Illinois know, Secretary Edgar has made a very high priority in our office of library activities and library business.

I'd like to give a special thanks to Eastern Illinois University today for it's coordinating efforts. As you know, Jim is a graduate of Eastern Illinois. In fact, I went to Harvard and found myself at somewhat of a disadvantage in our administration. Eastern Illinois is to the Jim Edgar administration as Harvard was to the John Kennedy administration. We've been quite fortunate really, that Jim during the course of his time there has been able to encourage a lot of people to be involved in Illinois State government—not only in the library but in other areas.

I live in Chicago and I work with some libraries here, so I do have an opportunity once in a while to address librarians. As a person who's an attorney and basically involved in all this for political reasons (I hate to throw a word like "politics" out at a group like this on Monday morning) but the fact is, I think this kind of activity and the leadership that Secretary Edgar has shown shows the benefits and the necessity for good political leadership. It also shows another thing with respect to libraries which make them so important to me. That is, I'm able to put libraries from my point of perspective, I think, in a larger context many times more easily than people who spend their lives working in libraries. I live in Des Plaines and we have a great public library. I know the head of the library and the

© 1985 by The Haworth Press, Inc. All rights reserved.

WAYNE ANDERSON: "Thomas Flexner . . . wrote some good things about libraries. He said libraries are the memory of mankind and if all the institutions on the Earth were destroyed, but we had a good library left, all of that could be recreated. But, if libraries were destroyed, all the accumulated wisdom in history could not be recreated. Each human being would have to discover it all over again."

people on the library board, and their lives very much get caught up in circulation figures, and our new computerized library cards. I was in the library yesterday, but the line was so long I managed to use my old card for one last time. These mechanical things are really important. But, from a larger perspective of all of society, I think we can hardly overestimate the importance of libraries. At the risk of duplicating some things that you already know, and which probably really got you involved in library work, I'd like to set what I think is the tone for this conference from the perspective of someone who's not a librarian, but who thinks libraries are very important.

Probably, the major thing that distinguishes us as human beings from any other of God's creations is our ability to pass on information and to grow from generation to generation. When you think about it, libraries are the institutions that help us do that. Thomas Flexner who became even more famous this last week when his biography of Washington was put on TV, also wrote some good things about libraries. He said libraries are the memory of mankind and if all the institutions on the Earth were destroyed, but we had a good library left, all of that could be recreated. But if libraries were destroyed, all the accumulated wisdom in history could not be recreated. Each human being would have to discover it all over again.

As a politician and a government official, I see a lot of things that government tries to do and most of those things have a very dangerous downside. The costs are great, or you're helping this person and hurting that person—I've got to say that library work is one of the few things I've ever been involved in that has very little downside. If you think for a moment, the good that libraries do for individual human beings, I think it can make you feel very good about your whole life's work. Imagine what libraries do on a one-on-one basis. A father comes home from work and decides that he's going to stop off at the library and take out some books, for a three or four year old, to read with his child. Well, that experience enables that working parent, father or mother really, to grow up with the child. In our library in Des Plaines, we teach immigrants to this country English and set them really in our society. So the library becomes not just an enjoyable place for us but a place where American citizenship—and I think those are words perhaps we use too frivolously—the important *qualities* of American citizenship become available to people who are trying to become part of our society.

The list really is endless. Such as, the person who as a young child comes into the library, gets excited about a particular subject

WAYNE ANDERSON: "As a politician and a government official, I see a lot of things that government tries to do and most of those things have a very dangerous downside. . . . I've got to say that library work is one of the few things I've ever been involved in that has very little downside."

matter, then ten or twenty years later becomes a great physician, or a scientist, or a business leader. These are things which libraries do, that I think of really, as unmitigated good. There are very few institutions in our society that do unmitigated good.

I'd like to make a pitch for one particular cause when I have this moment before you; that's the cause of free speech. There's one thing that you're aware of as custodians of ideas. It's that ideas are probably the most important thing to human beings, and I think libraries have a more important role, perhaps even [more] than free governments, in maintaining the right to a free exchange of ideas, preserving ideas without judgment as to their merits. If we do these things, I think human beings as individuals as well as a group will ultimately continue to progress. I think libraries are indispensable for that.

I'm really pleased to be here today. Jim Edgar likes these functions so much that I rarely get to do this. I think he is wisely about 1,295 miles south of here at this moment and probably having a good time. But on behalf of both the Secretary of State and Eastern Illinois University, I want to welcome you and I hope you have a very good day.

Thank you very much.

WAYNE ANDERSON: "I'd like to make a pitch for one particular cause when I have this moment before you; that's the cause of free speech...ideas are probably the most important thing to human beings, and I think libraries have a more important role, perhaps even [more] than free governments, in maintaining the right to a free exchange of ideas, perserving ideas without judgment as to their merits.

MORNING SESSION

(Introductory Remarks by Bridget Lamont)

The strong commitment to library cooperation is based on a very aggressive state-based network—ILLINET. We cannot start this day without making special thanks and mention to Dr. Wilson Luquire, the Dean of Library Services at Eastern Illinois University. Wilson has taken a leadership role in Illinois and I think nationally, by coordinating these conferences. He has committed both his institution's resources and his own personal interest in library networking by making these programs available to all of us. We find they're particularly useful for the Illinois library community and those librarians who might not make it to a national conference by having something offered such as this in their own state. Wilson, we want to thank you for your efforts.

I think this kind of effort is really not unexpected in Illinois, given the kinds of commitment that we have shown in the past to library networking. This conference is being co-sponsored by a number of library organizations in Illinois as well. I started my remarks yesterday on the plane, and after having dinner with a number of our speakers, I scrapped all of them. I tried to jot down a few opening comments for you. I've also scratched my comments by at least 50% because they all have so much to say and they want to get right at it. I think it's going to be a real challenge to be coordinating the efforts today.

This promises to be a particularly provocative discussion, and from what I understand, it appears to me as though the off-the-cuff comments that you'll be hearing perhaps before, during, and after the speeches may be the most fascinating part of the program today. Last night at cocktails, before dinner, during dinner, and I understand there were some who stayed up very late, we heard talk of entrepreneurs; discussions over what really is a network; the personalities that contribute or impede networking success; the impact of library cooperation and the impact of library competition; the levels of competition that might exist in the library network; the key factors of governance and who's got the money; and the promise for regional networking. I think that we'll be hearing comments on many of these points today.

A few housekeeping details: first of all, John Linford will be unable to join us today to talk about the NELINET Experience. That provides the rest of our speakers a little more time for off-the-cuff comments or repartee based on what they're hearing each other say. (No one could get their hands on the written speeches, even last night. So, we're waiting to hear what's really going to occur.) We will then move the afternoon break up accordingly, and we will start our panel discussion/questions from the audience a little bit earlier in the program than we had originally planned. I think that that's good and bad. For those people who are trying to fly out of Chicago today, they can watch the fog and maybe it will clear, and it will allow us a little bit more time for questions, answers and just general discussion.

The order of the program . . . the speakers will follow just as they are listed in the program. I'm still not sure how Wilson put the list of speakers together. Originally, it seemed to me, that we worked towards the national and international experiences. But after talking with some members of the panel last night, they thought that perhaps people were listed according to their age—or at least by wisdom. So we'll wait to see what they all do today. Those of us in Illinois, who know Al Trezza just assumed that he had demanded to have the last comments, but I do know that some of his colleagues intend to say a lot more after Al finishes today anyway, so we'll see.

The AMIGOS Experience: Development of a Successful Network

James H. Kennedy

Western Region Marketing Manager
OCLC, Inc.
Dublin, Ohio

(Introductory Remarks by Bridget Lamont)

Our first speaker is Jim Kennedy, currently the Marketing Manager for the Western Region for OCLC's local systems. He was Executive Director of AMIGOS (a very, very nationally recognized regional library network for eight years), and led that not-for-profit network into a very active program. Programs of which were used, not only by that part of the country, but by other libraries as well. Jim's experience as an operations manager for Richard Abell and a system's analyst for the Planning Research Company contributed, I believe, to his success as a network director. During his tenure in AMIGOS, he was known for marketing computer based information services to libraries and city governments in five states and Latin America.
Jim Kennedy.

* * *

I'm just hoping the weather does improve so that I can get back to marketing OCLC local systems. I'm reminded by talking with Bridget and so forth that people often say, "Well, being a network director is really a political job." So therefore, I have to assume that they mean that I must have been somewhat of a politician. Well, I don't really think so because the definition of a politician—one definition—is someone who can tell you to go to hell with such tact that you look forward to the trip. I never could do that.

So, I'm here today to tell you a little bit about the background of AMIGOS; how it was organized and what perhaps made it successful. It's very difficult for me to be the judge of that. You all would have to be the judge. Also, it being a regional network of five states (and maybe Latin America if the monetary situation was a little better), may not translate into activities that you in Illinois and the midwest enjoy. But, I want to give you some of the background. Of course, all of this is history because as you'll see, certain things happen, I believe, because there were certain things not in place or in place that if you were to do it today, you would do it differently. But that, like somebody says, is 20/20 hindsight.

The AMIGOS Bibliographic Council, Inc. is a library network agency serving libraries in Arizona, Kansas, Louisiana, New Mexico, Oklahoma, and Texas. Utilizing this organization, libraries are engaged in a variety of resource sharing activities and services to improve library services.

AMIGOS is not an acronym, but just a Spanish word meaning "friends." For those readers who insist on having an acronym, AMIGOS could be interpreted to mean "Association of Member Institutions Giving Online Services."

In either case, AMIGOS has typified this meaning, namely to provide unique and excellent services to libraries throughout the United Stated and Latin America, and at the same time promote resource sharing. Based on the AMIGOS "1983 Annual Report,"[1] the organization's net assets were in excess of $1.4 million! If this is used as a measure of success, then this agency is one of the most successful library networks in the country.

What is the reason for this success? Is it due to its governance, its staff, its services and products, or the AMIGOS member libraries? Following is an examination of these factors.

GOVERNANCE

The organization originated from libraries of the institutions belonging to the Interuniversity Council of North Texas (IUC). In early 1973, a meeting of interested parties was held to determine the feasibility of utilizing the developing Ohio College Library Center (OCLC) to serve libraries in the North Central Texas area. Under the guidance of the Bibliographic Network Committee (BNC) of the IUC, an IUC/OCLC relationship was established in October 1973 for 13 IUC institutions and 6 other libraries in Texas and New Mexico. A grant was obtained from the Texas State Library to permit 3 public libraries, a school district library, and the State Library to participate in the IUC/OCLC network. Thus, by early 1974, the network of 24 libraries represented large and small, private and public academic libraries; large and small public libraries; medical libraries; a school district's libraries and a State Library. Also, the BNC was enlarged to provide representation for these new non-IUC libraries—one representative each from the western and southern sectors of the network.

Based upon interest from other libraries in OCLC, the BNC distributed a questionnaire to ascertain the level of interest in expanding the IUC/OCLC network into a southwestern network. Results of the questionnaire plus consideration of other issues relating to network expansion (such as staffing, terminal maintenance, and governance), led to preparation of a tentative proposal for expansion which was approved at a BNC meeting in November 1974. The BNC recommended to IUC members a structure that would place the responsibility for operation of the expanded network in a new organization, composed of representatives from each participating library, and network staff under the umbrella of the IUC Board of Directors. The latter agency was chosen because of its charter, tax status, and bank financing. This would enable the new network to become operational as soon as possible.[2]

Approval of the expansion plan by the IUC resulted in creation of the AMIGOS Bibliographic Council. The bylaws of the new organization stated that AMIGOS would have its own Executive Director, staff, and Executive Board elected by the member libraries, all of whom fell under the authority of the IUC Board of Directors. These bylaws were approved by the library members at their initial meeting on May 29, 1975 and by the IUC Board at their June 17, 1975 meeting.

This governance structure proved to be unwieldy. For example: AMIGOS library members or staff would make recommendations to the AMIGOS Executive Board; Executive Board recommendations would then be submitted to the IUC Board of Directors (Presidents of the IUC institutions) for approval. Thus, the possibility existed for the IUC Board to deny a program which was desired by the member libraries. Furthermore, as the network expanded and ac-

16   *EXPERIENCES OF LIBRARY NETWORK ADMINISTRATORS*

JAMES H. KENNEDY: "Approval of the expansion plan by the IUC resulted in creation of the AMIGOS Bibliographic Council. The bylaws of the new organization stated that AMIGOS would have its own Executive Director, staff, and Executive Board elected by the member libraries, all of whom fell under the authority of the IUC Board of Directors. . . .
This governance structure proved to be unwieldy."

quired more library members outside of the North Central Texas region, the AMIGOS membership felt that IUC institutions had undue control, considering the diverse needs of AMIGOS libraries.

Because of these concerns, as well as expanded services and liabilities of AMIGOS, the IUC Board initiated procedures in 1978 for establishing AMIGOS as an independent network agency. Thus, on July 1, 1979 the AMIGOS Bibliographic Council, Inc. became a separate legal entity representing approximately 145 libraries in the Southwest.

The new bylaws of AMIGOS reflected a different governance structure. Namely, a Board of Trustees composed of 12 members, 9 of which were elected from among the official voting representatives of AMIGOS, and 3 members elected from persons active in civic, private, or institutional management. The Board of Trustees had corporate authority and control over all affairs of AMIGOS. However, all actions of the Board were subject to review by the membership.

Each AMIGOS member library had one vote on issues and policies presented to them at membership meetings. This meant that small and large libraries had the same rights and interests—sometimes a concern for large member libraries. Furthermore, AMIGOS members could vote to levy dues, fees, etc. upon themselves, even though the Board of Trustees approved the organization's budget. Since the fees and budget were intertwined, this split in responsibility sometimes created problems.

Success of the organization can be attributed partly to contributions made by AMIGOS members who served on the Board of Trustees, the former Executive Board and the Bibliographic Network Committee. These Boards permitted the network staff to operate the day-to-day activities and supported a majority of the staff's recommended policies and new services. Board members attempted to represent all types and sizes of libraries when considering new services, policies, and fees.

STAFF

After the contract between the IUC and OCLC was negotiated in late 1973, the IUC hired Barbara Gates to provide OCLC profiling and training services for the initial 24 libraries. A small IUC/ TAGER (The Association for Graduate Education and Research)

JAMES H. KENNEDY: "Each AMIGOS member library had one vote on issues and policies presented to them at membership meetings. This meant that small and large libraries had the same rights and interests—sometimes a concern for large member libraries. Furthermore, AMIGOS members could vote to levy dues, fees, etc. upon themselves, even though the Board of Trustees approved the organization's budget. Since the fees and budget were intertwined, this split in responsibility sometimes created problems."

administrative staff, supported by network and grant funds, performed the required administrative, accounting, and terminal maintenance functions (OCLC could not provide this service at that time). Since it was imperative that all libraries become operational as soon as possible, this small staff provided high quality service under sometimes difficult conditions.

In early 1975, the AMIGOS Bibliographic Council hired its initial Executive Director, James H. Kennedy. He was selected because of his broad background and experience with libraries, automation in the public and private sector, library networks, and library jobbers. The initial tasks of the Executive Director were to create a service-oriented organization with sufficient staff. At the same time, the Executive Director had to develop new programs, and to further the OCLC training program.

In order to provide OCLC services to more than 30 new libraries in each of the next four years, AMIGOS hired several more trainers (Library Liaison Officers (LLO's)). AMIGOS member libraries required experienced LLO's (at least 3 years technical services experience) in order to perform OCLC training. In addition to knowing library and OCLC systems, LLO's had to be willing to travel and be able to demonstrate the OCLC system at individual library sites.

AMIGOS also recognized that financial management of its funds received from member libraries for services was critical to a viable organization. To this end, unlike other network agencies, AMIGOS hired and retained an experienced business manager to manage and invest AMIGOS' funds and advise the Executive Director. This concentration on fiscal affairs was a major factor in making AMIGOS a financial success.

In addition to having excellent staff, AMIGOS organized its operations so that a senior staff member was responsible for each major cost and profit center. This helped focus tasks and functions in order to maintain cost-effective services while providing close budget control.

PRODUCTS/SERVICES

As mentioned previously, the AMIGOS Bibliographic Council was established to provide libraries with an interconnection to the OCLC online catalog subsystem. AMOGOS charged fees to library members for this service of profiling, training, terminal maintenance, and finance management. Thus, services had to be of sufficiently high quality for the libraries to continue to pay these additional fees.

In the initial years of AMIGOS, OCLC did not provide adequate training support and documentation. To offset this deficiency, AMIGOS generated additional publications to assist the libraries. Through its quarterly newsletter and its monthly technical newsletter, "Bits & Tidbits," AMIGOS attempted to inform its members of the activities of other networks, library news, and provide other information of interest to technical services staff.

To provide in-depth coverage of OCLC subsystems, each Library Liaison Officer was assigned special areas of responsibility. Incoming information and member queries were then routed to the specialist in that area. Training responsibilities were also reallocated along the same lines. Thus, as more OCLC subsystems were added, AMIGOS added more LLO trainers. A major feature of AMIGOS' OCLC services was to conduct all profiling and training at the libraries' sites.

Workshops were held on various topics throughout the Southwest so the AMIGOS libraries could utilize the OCLC system in a cost-efficient manner. For example, in 1980 and 1981, workshops were conducted on Interlibrary Loan concerns, OCLC/MARC formats for serials and non-book materials, and on utilization of AACR2.

As OCLC developed more subsystems, AMIGOS determined that it was in the best interest of its members to promote these new functions. Due to "crash" training sessions in 1979, AMIGOS libraries were consistently using the OCLC ILL subsystem as borrowers at a higher rate than libraries of other Networks (usually 20-25% of all OCLC ILL requests were placed by AMIGOS libraries).

Also, after OCLC implemented the Acquisitions subsystem in 1981, AMIGOS conducted a series of 10 workshops in order to promote its use by member libraries. By July 1982, AMIGOS members' total usage represented about 40% of the total OCLC Acquisitions subsystem activity—another result of active training and marketing.

In addition to training libraries about the intricate features of the OCLC systems, libraries had questions about terminals, printers, cables, and magnetic tapes. AMIGOS felt that technical information should be provided on an on-going basis. As a by-product of developing this data, AMIGOS sold "slave" printers and terminal/modem cables at a discount price both to AMIGOS libraries and to other libraries in the United States.

AMIGOS provided consulting services to libraries in the Southwest and also Latin America. After many years of discussions with various libraries in Mexico, two libraries joined AMIGOS and began using OCLC. Unfortunately, the Mexican monetary system made the use of the OCLC system impractical during 1983 and 1984. AMIGOS may offer Latin American libraries other data processing alternatives in the near future.

As a by-product of using the OCLC cataloging subsystem, libraries were able to receive their bibliographic records in machine-readable form in the MARC format. In 1976 or 1977, OCLC provided these cataloging records for groups of libraries. AMIGOS felt that these tape records of its members' cataloging could be a future resource for the AMIGOS members.

Thus, AMIGOS developed a Tape Service, based on a monthly subscription tape containing all AMIGOS' cataloging records. Using computers and staff at The University of Texas at Dallas, copies of the tapes were made for permanent storage and tapes containing an extraction of catalog records were made for library subscribers. Also, special tape extractions, such as data for use in numeric registers and name authority systems were prepared. This service was the basis for AMIGOS' current data processing activities.

Another by-product service utilizing the OCLC tapes enable libraries to create Computer Output Microform (COM) catalogs. By special arrangement with a COM vendor, Brodart, AMIGOS offered COM services tailored to individual library requirements at special discounted prices.

In an attempt to provide additional discounts for library services, AMIGOS signed a contract with Bibliographic Retrieval Services (BRS) in 1978. Unlike some networks, AMIGOS did not provide training or searching of BRS' data bases—just discounted fees. Later AMIGOS offered discounts for another online reference service, DIALOG.

Although OCLC services continued to occupy the majority of AMIGOS staff time, AMIGOS was beginning to broker services of other organizations whenever they filled the needs of AMIGOS member libraries. Furthermore, for AMIGOS to be a viable organization, the members did not want it to be dependent on any one service or product. Goal 1 of the "AMIGOS Long-Range Plan"[3] states: "Provide computerized library services and products to all types of libraries in the AMIGOS region in order to implement cooperative library programs in a cost-effective and cost-efficient manner." Goal 3 of the "Plan" states: "Become the leading service agency for libraries in the AMIGOS region specializing in computerized network services while avoiding dependency on any one library vendor or organization for its services." To this end, in 1980 AMIGOS began to offer services that were complementary to those provided by OCLC.

In addition to processing the OCLC multi-institutional tapes for AMIGOS member libraries, AMIGOS established a cataloging and retrospective conversion service utilizing the OCLC online cataloging subsystem. Individual libraries desiring to convert their catalog records into machine readable format or catalog new material could contract with AMIGOS to undertake these keyboarding and cataloging functions. AMIGOS provided staff to search the OCLC data base and modify necessary data for the library. This service was begun in 1980 and has now been expanded to any libraries in the United States that wish to participate. Thus far, over 100 libraries have used this service.

Because of the impact of data processing technology on libraries and the likelihood that more and more libraries would acquire their computer systems, AMIGOS determined that it should assist libraries toward more effective use of this technology. In late 1980, results of a questionnaire regarding the AMIGOS Tape Extraction Service provided the basis for a recommendation to the AMIGOS Board of Trustees that AMIGOS acquire in-house processing capability. The AMIGOS Board, not wanting to duplicate SOLINET's data processing problems and expenses, approved the acquisition of a medium-size minicomputer from Tandem Computers, Inc. The initial goal was to enhance the AMIGOS tape extraction service. As this service was being improved, AMIGOS began using the computer for in-house financial processing and control, and began investigating possible on-line services.

As a by-product of the tape extraction activities, AMIGOS offered new services during 1982-1983, namely, AACR2 conversion, as well as file conversion of OCLC/MARC records to file formats of CLSI, Dataphase, and other systems. In addition to processing AMIGOS' libraries' tapes, AMIGOS maintained tape records for BCR, NELINET and PALINET libraries.

In order to improve and offer a more cost-effective retrospective conversion process for libraries, AMIGOS acquired some Tandem Computer software programs developed by the University of California at Berkeley Library. These programs provided the capability to modify OCLC/MARC records online. Based on successful demonstrations in October 1983, the AMIGOS Board of Trustees approved implementation of the AMIGOS SHARES (SHAred REsource System) program—an online retrospective conversion system utilizing the AMIGOS data base. The operational system provides low cost, high quality records utilizing full screen editing and extensive use of function keys. This expedited editing, thus reducing conversion costs to the libraries.

MEMBER LIBRARIES

The AMIGOS member libraries' participation in the organization's activities made the network stronger. The library representatives attended semi-annual technical sessions and membership meetings, budget hearings, interlibrary loan meetings. At these latter meetings, they produced and adopted a regional ILL Code establishing protocols among AMIGOS members for mutual loans at no charge.

With this varied input from different types and sizes of libraries, the AMIGOS staff and Board were able to structure products and services for the member library users. This input created a responsive library network organization.

SUMMARY

Although the AMIGOS Bibliographic Council, Inc. has been a very successful network, can they maintain that position? Based on the factors of governance, staff, programs and services, and library members, AMIGOS should be able to continue as a powerful library agency in the Southwest. However, there are many forces that may have an effect on AMIGOS' growth. Some of these factors are: (a) OCLC's new "local systems" products, (b) microcomputers, (c) new storage technology, (d) less use of large cataloging data bases, (e) new library products, (f) the need for continued research and development to generate new products for AMIGOS members and other libraries, and (g) limited library funds.

The initial years of the AMIGOS network were exciting, risk-taking ones. The AMIGOS organization and its services have created a new bond between libraries in the Southwest. Hopefully, the

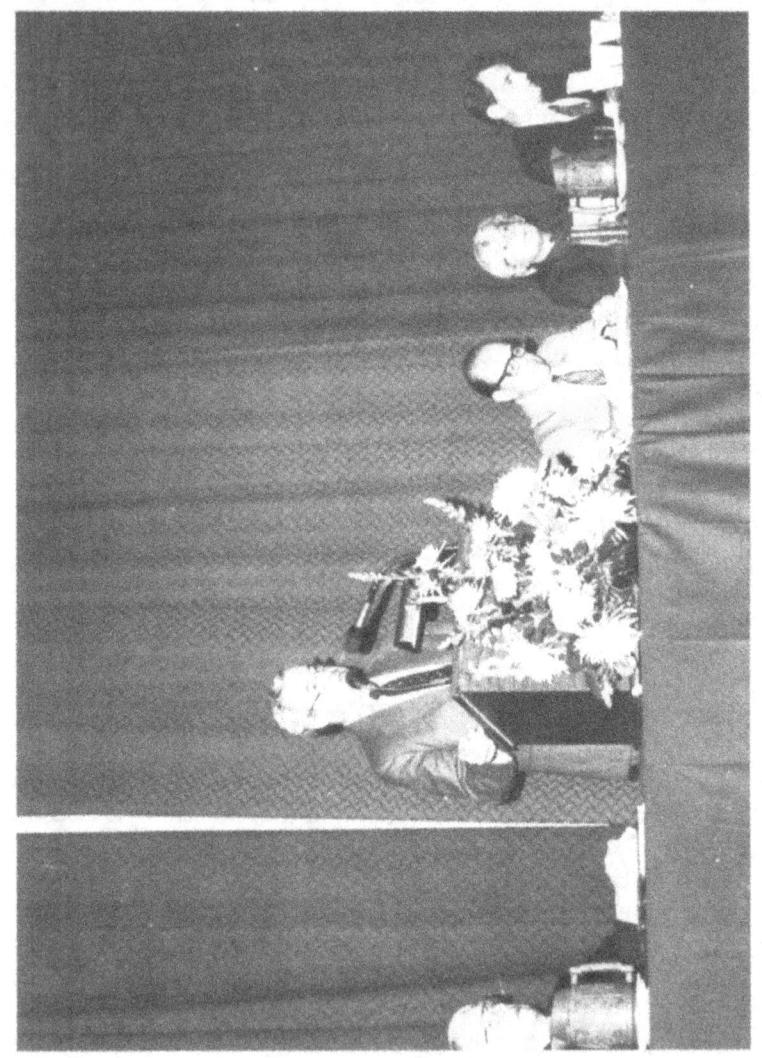

JAMES H. KENNEDY: "Because of the impact of data processing technology on libraries and the likelihood that more and more libraries would acquire their computer systems, AMIGOS determined that it should assist libraries toward more effective use of this technology."

member libraries, Board of Trustees, and staff of AMIGOS can continue this service and resource sharing for library users in the future by developing new cost-efficient products. With increased marketing and development of services, AMIGOS should be a very strong and viable library network organization during the next five (5) years.

REFERENCES

1. "1983 Annual Report" (1984?): 10-11.
2. "A Proposal for the Expansion of the IUC/OCLC Network" (1974?): 9-10.
3. "Annual Report 1981" (1982?): 3.

Library Networks Circa 1984 or One Blind Person Touching the Elephant

Alice E. Wilcox

Reference Division
University of Minnesota Libraries
Minneapolis, Minnesota

(Introductory Remarks by Bridget Lamont)

Alice Wilcox is a member of the Reference Division at the University of Minnesota but, perhaps best known for her experience as Director of MINITEX for thirteen years. Alice is certainly well recognized for her leadership in serials access projects. In our conversations last night, it appears to me as though she has a particular interest and most definite thoughts about what I call "the network personality" and the impact of that personality in cooperative library networks. Her numerous activities include being a member of the Nicholas Task Force on Periodical Systems, and her work as a member of the Advisory Committee for the Pre-White House Conference on Networks. Because of the relative geographic proximity of Minnesota to Illinois and since both are state-based networks, many of us in Illinois have followed MINITEX's activities. Although, I think libraries throughout the country have benefited from the leadership role and Ms. Wilcox's work in the area of serials control. Alice.

* * *

Thank you. It's a pleasure to be here this morning. Firstly, I think I'm the only one of our speakers today—you'll notice they're all men and I think all of them are wearing what's close to a pin-stripe suit. I don't know what that really says, but I think it says something. The second thing is that contrary to the reputation of most of my gender, I probably will have the shortest remarks, because I know my colleagues up here all have a lot to say and like to say a lot. And I don't like to do either one. But, nevertheless . . . What I'd like to do this morning is talk about "Library Networks Circa 1984 or One Blind Person Touching the Elephant."

The geography of the toucher determines the perceptions in the original East Indian tale. In order to somewhat appreciate my perspective, it might be useful to know something about the geography of the upper Midwest and specifically Minnesota. Three threads weave through our history and color our attitudes.

1. There is a long tradition of solving sticky problems thru cooperation and coalitions. Examples include: Minnesotans may be able to vote for Walter Mondale in November, but it will be on the Democratic Farmer Labor ticket; one of our Fortune 500 companies—Land of Lakes—is a farmer cooperative formed to market dairy products in the Eastern U.S.; and a coalition of business leaders transformed downtown Minneapolis into a vibrant growing commercial and shopping area. Today business and government are collaborators, not adversaries.
2. There is a strong commitment to education—public and private, elementary, secondary and post secondary. This egalitarian attitude began with the early settlers who believed education was their key to success—better paying and more meaningful employment, full participation in the political process and the opportunity to enhance their life thru quality leisure activities—and they were willing to make the necessary sacrifices. Today public monies provide grants and loans to all eligible applicants to attend any accredited post secondary institution in Minnesota.
3. There is a history of grass roots political participation. Independent ideas from many sources produce requests for enabling legislation and tax support. The peace corps started in a precinct caucus resolution that worked its way up to the National Democratic platform.

These three threads—cooperation and coalitions are the means to solve sticky problems, educational opportunities provide the pass-

ALICE E. WILCOX: "In order to somewhat appreciate my perspective, it might be useful to know something about the geography of the upper Midwest and specifically Minnesota. Three threads weave throughout history and color our attitudes. . . .

These threads—cooperation and coalitions are the means to solve sticky problems, educational opportunities provide the passport to the good life, and the perception that government is an enabling agency—color my perceptions."

port to the good life, and the perception that government is an enabling agency—color my perceptions.

In my alloted time I will try to discuss why the 1960's environment was conducive to library networking, specifically describe the focus and structure of MINITEX, make some observations regarding the impact of networking on the library community, suggest some lost opportunities and conclude with some comments on the "confusing Cs."

ENVIRONMENT CONDUCIVE TO NETWORKING

In the 1960's, all across the country, trouble was brewing in our libraries. On the one hand the publication explosion was filling our buildings faster than they could be built and the unit costs for organizing this material was simply out of control. As our society rapidly moved into an advanced technological state, its dependence upon information grew exponentially. The great society preached that access to information is an individual right and a societal responsibility. Meanwhile, both government and institutions, constrained by their increased commitments and a costly war, were forced to reduce their financial support to libraries. In addition, for the first time, as a nation, we began to understand finiteness and accept the realities of limited space and resources. Our immense national and library commitments and expectations exceeded our fiscal, natural and human resources. Innovative means were needed to increase access to library materials and stabilize or reduce the costs of buildings and processing. The magnitude of the data required utilization of electronic data processing. While the profession discussed the problem and talked about a national network, librarians formed groups (networks) to do the following:

a) develop or utilize a bibliographic utility, and or
b) provide increased access to library materials thru sharing their resources with each other.

The demographics of the libraries and their users tended to determine the priority focus, while the environment and personalities determined the structure. Libraries of nearly equal size and in close proximity obtain the greatest benefits from cooperative processing. In libraries scattered over large areas and of unequal size, the big-

ALICE E. WILCOX: "In the 1960's, all across the country, trouble was brewing in our libraries. On the one hand the publication explosion was filling our buildings faster than they could be built and the unit costs for organizing this material was simply out of control."

gest benefits come from resources sharing. While the National Library of Medicine developed an extensive resource sharing network, Ohio academic libraries jointly developed an online cataloging system. AMIGOS, INCOLSA, FEDLINK, PALINET, etc. were established to utilize a bibliographic utility.

Independent of any grand plan, and within less than a decade, the continental U.S. was covered with regional and state library networks. Thousands of formerly independent libraries voluntarily chose interdependent relationships and joined a network. Startling decisions were made regarding bibliographic and physical access to their collections. The magnitude of this rapid change was an amazing phenomenon.

MINITEX FOCUS AND STRUCTURE

In 1968 the State of Minnesota had several unique characteristics. The U of M was the only publicly supported university. There was no major private university in the state. The U of M's 3.4 million cataloged volumes nearly equaled the combined total of all the rest of post secondary education libraries and was almost 3 times as large as the state's largest public library. Over 3/4 of the state library resources were located in the Twin Cities metropolitan area. Ten years of Legislative catch-up library materials appropriations had made little progress. Any viable network in Minnesota required access to the University collection and then active participation. However, there was no known example of a major research library assuming the responsibilities of extensive resource sharing statewide. It was clearly easier to identify the problem—equity of library resources—than to solve it.

Beginning Jan. 1, 1969, a 2 year grant supported a pilot demonstration project to test the feasibility of sharing the university collection. Its primary purposes were to:

1. determine if materials could be supplied in a format and a time frame to be useful to out-of-state patrons,
2. measure the comparative costs of duplicating versus sharing collection, and
3. monitor the effect upon the primary users (university faculty and students).

ALICE E. WILCOX: "While the profession discussed the problem and talked about a national network, librarians formed groups (networks)... The demographics of the libraries and their users tended to determine the priority focus, while the environment and personalities determined the structure."

The results of the experiment provided convincing evidence that a state-supported sharing program would be practicable, economical and of considerable benefit to the state without undue determinant effects in the service to the University faculty and students. July 1, 1971 under the aegis of the Minnesota Higher Education Coordinating Board (MHECB), MINITEX was funded by the legislature to support academic participation. Additional state and federal LSCA monies supported public library participation. As a state program, it would have an advisory committee, but no governing body, a confusing situation for librarians. Responsibility for the program would reside with MHECB and they would contract with the university for facilities and administrative support. I believe that it was a good political decision that was educationally and economically sound.

Because 75% of the requested materials were for journal articles, the network decided in 1971 to begin building a data base of serials and only in 1976 did they begin building a common data base of monographs thru OCLC. One of their requirements was a contract allowing a machine readable tape of their records.

OBSERVATIONS REGARDING THE IMPACT OF NETWORKING ON THE LIBRARY COMMUNITY

1. Librarians at all levels learned to work together with significant attitudinal changes from independence to multi interdependencies.
2. There was rapid technology transfer in a tradition-bound labor intensive profession. Networkers, like the circuit-riding preachers, visited the hinterland, gathered librarians for meetings to teach the troops and recruit converts. Without a resident teacher, the locals assumed responsibilities for helping each other.
3. A profession already dependent upon standards developed a deeper appreciation for standards.
4. Identified excellence in cataloging and unique collections as they became visible on computer terminals.
5. Raised user expectations as it became reasonable to go to the local library and receive the needed item, be referred to a holding library, or have the item secured in their behalf.
6. Expanded the ability to do research and offer new courses in non-research institutions.

ALICE E. WILCOX: "Any viable network in Minnesota required access to the University collection and then active participation. However, there was no known example of a major research library assuming the responsibilities of extensive resource sharing statewide. It was clearly easier to identify the problem—equity of library resources—than to solve it."

7. Democratized the profession as leadership was expanded from professional organization officers to network responsibilities for major management decisions in member libraries. New leaders emerged. They weren't always the directors of the largest libraries. This was especially true in the second round of elections. The new power groups were sometimes threatening. Some people reverted to sandlot baseball tactics. When they didn't like the rules or leadership, they picked up their bats and balls (resources) and started a new group where they would be in control.
8. Provided useful statistical data that changed staffing patterns and collection development policy. For the first time, many libraries had reliable data on their demand for unowned materials.
9. Discovered that high cost of meetings swallowed some of the savings. With all of our technology, why must we travel so far and meet so often to accomplish so little?
10. Learned that resource sharing makes substantive changes in the local library. Ultimately it is the local library that will share its resources and become dependent upon the collection in other libraries.

LOST OPPORTUNITIES

1. We frequently lost the opportunity to use library automation to rethink the total library system instead of providing tools to perform specific tasks. Planning for automation should include a process to reassert and/or redefine the mission of the individual library. It should include asking what are we trying to do and how can we utilize new technology instead of how to automate. Automation will necessitate procedural and organizational change.
2. We lost the opportunity to maintain a healthy balance between the public and private sector. Instead of appreciating the unique roles and contributions of each, we blurred the distinctions. We failed to understand the difference between being businesslike and being a business. In addition to sitting on the sidelines as observers, we have often participated in the diminution of the not-for-profit sector. Witness the member/OCLC relationship change from cooperative to vendor. Witness the profes-

ALICE E. WILCOX: "Planning for automation should include a process to reassert and/or redefine the mission of the individual library. It should include asking what are we trying to do and how can we utilize new technology instead of how to automate. Automation will necessitate procedural and organizational change."

sional migration to the marketing arm of the corporation specializing in library products and services.
3. We lost the opportunity to coalesce our energies and resources to exert pressure on the marketplace. This failure has made us dependent on equipment manufactured for business and industry and subject to less than favorable pricing. Witness the tragic finale of the AD HOC Online Catalog Group that broke ranks at the critical bid proposal stage. Impatience, personal agendas, and lack of confidence destroyed our collective strength.
4. We lost the opportunity to provide the forum to bring together the computer and communication networks. Networking made us equally dependent upon both groups and our failure made us vulnerable to being held hostage to unacceptable price increases. Now we are faced with the new specter of IBM's going to bed with Phillips and AT&T entering the computer field. Of course, it's only speculation, but I prefer to believe that with statemanship we might have pulled it off 10 years ago.

THEN THERE ARE THE "CONFUSING Cs"

Coalesce - to unite by growth into one body
Collaborate - to work or act jointly
Community - A body of people having common organization or interests
Compete - to contend for the same position, reward for which another is striving
Concern - Interest in or care for others
Conduce - to lead or make for some (usually desirable) result
Control - to exercise restraint
Cooperate - to act or operate together
Create - to bring into being

The future of library networking may depend upon our choice of these "confusing Cs." There is a difference between choosing to coalesce to create an environment that is conducive to cooperative and collaborative activity, and choosing to compete for resources by controlling our constituency, abandoning our common concerns and allowing our lack of civility to destroy our community.

ALICE E. WILCOX: "We lost the opportunity to coalesce our energies and resources to exert pressure on the marketplace. This failure has made us dependent on equipment manufactured for business and industry and subject to less than favorable pricing."

We might consider the latest findings of the paleoanthropologists. New theories hold that cooperation, not competition divided man from ape.

CONCLUSION

The library community has been strengthened and raised to new heights when commonly stated goals and objectives have led to mutual respect and trust. Conversely, suspicion, mistrust and personal agendas have been disruptive and destructive.

* * *

Bridget Lamont

I don't know what Wilson told all of you, I've never worked with a group and this is the second year I've been at one of these panels where people not only keep the time that's been allotted to them, but take time. I think you've all got something really planned for the panel remarks this afternoon. We'll take a brief break and convene again at eleven or shortly thereafter.

The CLASS Experience

J. Michael Bruer

Director of Marketing
Carlyle Systems, Inc.
Berkeley, California

(Introductory Remarks by Bridget Lamont)

Mind you, that the theme of this program is "From Our Past: Toward 2000." And the speakers were asked to develop their comments based on their own personal experiences with a network organization. This in no way minimizes their current activities. Our next speaker, Michael Bruer, was formerly the Associate Director of the California Library Authority for Systems and Services, commonly referred to as CLASS. I still have my "California has CLASS" button in my collection. Michael is currently the Manager of Customer Support for Carlyle Systems, which is an organization which markets an online public access catalog as well as other library automated systems. Mr. Bruer has been the recipient of numerous awards including a Council of Library Resources fellowship. During his tenure as Associate Director of CLASS, he had primary responsibility for day by day management of services and the initiation of numerous innovative programs and projects. Although we hear library networks talk often of money crises, etc., I found it interesting in looking over the resumes of our speakers that Michael's resume specifically included that he had primary responsibility for fund raising activities. His skills include speeches, publications in the area of library materials conservation, and he has the ability to speak five languages, which certainly impressed me—Greek and Latin, French, German and Russian. Michael was relatively quiet at dinner although I know I faded earlier last night than many of our speakers did. But, from time to time, he'd pull out a little piece of paper and jot something down. So I want to see what you're really going to do with your remarks.

Michael Bruer.

* * *

Thank you, Bridget. It's a pleasure to be here. Based on the comments that we heard earlier from Alice, I feel constrained to justify my three-piece pin-stripe suit. There's a time and a place for everything I suppose. My own justification would be that it's a concession to Eastern Conservatism.

Last week I was attending the New Mexico Library Association meeting in Albuquerque, and found myself on the last night there in the company of Harry Broussard who is the Systems Librarian at University of New Mexico. He and I both favor good country music. So we went out into the wee hours to a local bar or "lounge" as they call it down there, and sat down to drink Jack Daniels and listen to country music. This bar was full of people all wearing cowboy boots, Levis, cowboy shirts, leather jackets, and so forth—except Old Bruer. I had on my three-piece pin-stipe suit from New York's Fifth Avenue.

> "There are two times in a man's life when he should not speculate: when he can't afford to and when he can."
>
> "Get your facts first, and then you can distort them as much as you please."
>
> *Mark Twain*

This paper opens with two quotations from Mark Twain which seem to me to be especially apropos to the present exigency. I will do my best to avoid distortion of the facts, but the subject is complex and the space allotted for exposition is necessarily compressed. Moreover, if an historical review of the CLASS experience is difficult and involved, with the consequent potential for factual deviation, speculation on the future of CLASS and of networking in general is even more problematic. The latter can not be avoided, however, if we are to place developments in their proper perspective, and I will therefore speculate briefly on one or two important points, whether I can afford it or not.

In the presentation that follows, there are two issues relevant to the CLASS experience that should be kept firmly in mind: (1) lessons learned about organizational behavior and product definition, and 2) lessons learned about governance methodology and decision-making complexity. I offer this caveat even though it was Mark Twain, once again, who suggested that one should "never learn to do anything; if you don't learn, you'll always find someone else to do it for you." This advice seems to me to be overly restrictive, and I am therefore more comfortable with Winston Churchill who remarked that he was personally always ready to learn, although he did not always like being taught. Be that as it may, the following historical overview of the CLASS experience will highlight those aspects of the organization and its governance which resulted in special problems and which ultimately led to equally special solutions. I will return to both of these issues in the context of a discussion of current major problems and potential directions in networking.

CLASS, the California Library Authority for Systems and Services, was officially established in 1976 under the terms and conditions of a State of California Joint Exercise of Powers Agreement (JEPA). The purpose of JEPA legislation is to provide a means for existing public agencies to combine their resources in a given area in order to achieve objectives that would be either impossible or uneconomic for any one of them acting individually. This formulation is somewhat akin to what many people think is meant by library cooperation. In the case of CLASS, the public agencies involved were: the University of California, the California State University and College System, the California State Library, the California State Community College System, the County of Santa Clara on behalf of county public libraries, and the City of Los Angeles on behalf of city public libraries. The Board of Directors consisted of the signatories to the JEPA representing the above named institutions: the President of the University of California, the Chancellor of the State College System, the State Librarian, the President of the Community College System, the Chief Administrative officer of the County of Santa Clara, and the Mayor of Los Angeles. In addition, the Board incorporated two non-voting members, elected by the member libraries representing institutions in the non-public sector, the private colleges and universities and the special libraries.

The purpose of the Joint Exercise of Powers Agreement, and by extension the purpose of CLASS, was to create an agency which would assist the parties in their joint efforts to develop and implement a system for library program development and resource sharing, with particular emphasis on the following objectives:

1. Provide for the cooperative development and maintenance of common bibliographic and holdings data bases;
2. Provide for development and implementation of an interlibrary loan and delivery system;
3. Provide for development and operation of systems for cooperative use of cataloging data, cooperative acquisitions, and other forms of resource sharing; and
4. Provide for the development and implementation of library systems for information exchange.

It must be admitted that there is a certain lack of specificity in this formulation of purpose, making it difficult to determine just what the mission of the organization was supposed to be. The JEPA was also not very helpful in defining how the organization would pay for its activity in that Section XVII on Financing consisted of a single sentence: "CLASS shall be self-supporting, deriving its revenue from grants and from payments for services rendered to the parties and other participating agencies."

From the beginning, CLASS policy was approved by the Board of Directors, voting members of which are appointed by the six signatories of the Joint Powers Agreement, the official instrument which provides a legal basis for CLASS's existence. The Board, in turn, was advised on most things by the Authority Advisory Council (AAC). The AAC was composed of twenty-one members who were elected by the CLASS membership, which was in turn represented in the Council of Members.

The membership was divided into Segments, which were roughly equivalent to types of libraries; i.e., public, special, community college, the University of California, the State University and College System, private academic, and the State Library. Each Segment elected a Convenor who served as its primary spokesperson. A list of the Convenors was published in each issue of the official newsletter *CLASSACTION,* later called *CLASSONLINE,* so that CLASS members and others could contact an appropriate representative as the need arose. The Convenors provided the members with a personal channel for communication about CLASS matters. Of course, anyone could contact a CLASS staff member or a member of the Board about any issue.

Other decision-making processes were undertaken by specially appointed task groups or committees. One of the most important of these groups was the Long-Range Planning Task Group, which had key responsibility in determining program definition and objectives and in formulating a long-range plan for the organization.

Specific services and products were developed within program areas recommended by the AAC and approved by the Board. The specifics of such products—format, pricing, content and the like—were devised by CLASS administrative staff with the advice of various advisory committees.

Here, it may be well to recall Fred Allen's definition of a committee: "A group of people who individually can do nothing, but as a group decide that nothing can be done." It has also been said that a committee is a group of the unfit, appointed by the unwilling, to do the unnecessary. While it may well be that these views represent overstatements, it nevertheless remains true that a complex committee structure adds greatly to an organization's overhead and, to a degree, impedes its ability to deal with important issues quickly and expeditiously, however much the democratic process may be served as a consequence. Equally important, the prospect of making the enterprise self-supporting, as required by the JEPA, is significantly jeopardized.

Many knotty problems were dealt with in various ways by this rather cumbersome organizational structure. One of them was the definition of membership criteria, including the development of an equitable formulation for public library systems participation. Since CLASS is a democratic organization, complex issues consumed much debate time before most people could be satisfied with the result.

Membership fees, for example, were originally set at $100 per institution per year. These fees were later revised to a sliding scale of $40-80-120 depending on the size of the library. Fees were raised gradually over the years, but are still among the lowest for an organization of the size and complexity of CLASS. Currently, fees are set at $85-150-225, again depending on library size as defined by the aggregate budget for books and other library materials averaged over a three year period.

Finally, in December 1977, the CLASS Board approved nine program areas within which CLASS would develop services and products. These program areas were initiated by the Authority Advisory Council with the help of CLASS staff and four task groups. The nine program area titles were as follows:

PROGRAM   I: The Cooperative Library Network
PROGRAM   II: The California Data Base (Monographs)
PROGRAM   III: The California Data Base (Serials)
PROGRAM   IV: Online Reference Services
PROGRAM   V: Communications and Delivery
PROGRAM   VI: Storage of Library Materials
PROGRAM VII: Conservation, Preservation, Restoration
PROGRAM VIII: Continuing Education
PROGRAM   IX: Technical Consulting

Members of the Authority Advisory Council met in 1978 to review CLASS's progress toward developing the programs and services recommended by the AAC in 1977. After intensive discussion of issues affecting CLASS's role and operations, the AAC made a number of recommendations to the CLASS Board of Directors. Key recommendations were:

> The AAC has reviewed the programs and services which CLASS has been developing and affirms their continued development.
> CLASS should develop a close liaison with the California Library Services Board (CLSB) and offer CLASS's services to the CLSB in that Board's public policy roles of promoting integration of library services. (The CLSB oversees distribution of several million dollars annually in state funds to promote public library cooperative services such as interlibrary loan.)
> CLASS should . . . pursue with CLSB the means for access to all California public library data bases, preferably under CLASS's technical management. (To a degree, both of the CLSB objectives were realized.)
> CLASS can most effectively help libraries deal with the effects of Proposition 13 by aggressively developing and promoting its programs which substantively anticipated Proposition 13. (It may be recalled that Prop 13, as it is known colloquially, was a tax measure approved by the California electorate that strictly limited the rate at which property taxes could be as-

sessed, with the result that the revenue base for local jurisdictions, including libraries, was greatly reduced.)

CLASS should pursue out-of-state cooperative/marketing endeavors that do not interfere with service to California.

CLASS should continue and intensify its involvement in the introduction of several bibliographic networks and utilities to California libraries, beginning with BALLOTS. (BALLOTS was subsequently renamed the Research Libraries Information Network, or RLIN, a major bibliographic utility provided by RLG, the Research Libraries Group.)

Events were to prove that some of these programs would never exist except on paper. Agreement was never reached, for example, on the meaning and objectives of Program V, Communications and Delivery, despite protracted efforts on the part of the membership and various advisory committees. Storage of Library Materials, Program VI, was put on hold pending developments associated with a major effort by the University of California to design and construct massive storage facilities in Northern and Southern California, primarily for the benefit of the nine university campuses. Funding was never secured for Conservation, Program VII, although a great deal of administrative time and effort was devoted to the problem. It was soon realized that Continuing Education, separately listed as Program VII, was an integral part of CLASS activities rather than a separate program as such. The definition of the Cooperative Library Network, Program I, became clear only after a contract was signed with Stanford (later RLG) for provision of BALLOTS (later RLIN) services to those libraries that were not members of RLG.

Ultimately, the "programs" that actually got underway came to be viewed rather more precisely as products and services, and there was a general consolidation into two main areas: data base services, including in particular the California Data Base for Monographs and the California Data Base for Serials (originally Programs II and III); and online services, including RLIN shared cataloging, the online reference operation (previously Program IV), as well as several entirely new services that were not envisioned when the nine original programs were established. These later online services included provision of the Ontyme electronic mail system, brokering of computer-related equipment, and development and distribution of microcomputer-based programs for library applications.

At the same time that program offerings were undergoing consolidation and re-orientation, special attention was also being given to organizational and planning issues. At their January 1979 meeting, the CLASS Board called upon the AAC to develop a long-range plan for CLASS. As a first step, existing plans within the segments were to be examined with a view to how well they meshed with each other to provide an intersegmental approach for improving California library service. The AAC segmental convenors, meeting later that January, accepted the Board's call, and agreed to provide nominations for a Long-Range Planning Task Group to be appointed at the March meeting of the AAC.

In August 1979, the CLASS Authority Advisory Council recommended the following amendment to the CLASS Bylaws, Article V, Section 3. This change would allow for the inclusion of out-of-state libraries in the segmental structure. Library segments which make up the Congress of Members would be redefined as follows:

ORIGINAL SEGMENT NAME	NEW SEGMENT NAME
The University of California Libraries	University libraries (to include all state universities which offer doctoral programs)
The California State University Colleges Libraries	State University and College Libraries (to include all state university and college libraries which offer Masters programs)
The Community College Libraries	Community College Libraries
The Public Libraries	Public Libraries
The State Library	State Libraries
Private Academic Libraries	Private Academic Libraries
Special Libraries	Special Libraries

The consequences of this apparently innocuous change in the bylaws were far-reaching indeed. On July 1, 1983, CLASS officially changed its name from the California Library Authority for Systems and Services to the Cooperative Library Agency for Systems and Services. The new name (which does not change the acronym) is a more accurate reflection of the nationwide orientation of CLASS.

CLASS was formed as an autonomous public agency that would act as the regional library network for the State of California. In the three years, 1980-83, the demand for CLASS's services from libraries outside California increased dramatically. With over five hundred members from coast to coast and thousands of customers, use of "California" in the official name became anachronistic. In addition, CLASS has no jurisdiction responsibilities as the term "Authority" suggests. The CLASS Board believed that the name change would help make the purpose of CLASS easier to interpret to the library community.

Meanwhile, throughout 1979 the AAC, with the leadership of the Long-Range Planning Task Group, continued work on the modification of a long-range plan for the organization. Parts I and IV of CLASS 1984: THE FIVE YEAR PLAN were approved by the Board on December 10, 1979, the two completed parts being PART I: GOALS, OBJECTIVES, IMPLEMENTATION PHASES and PART IV: APPENDICES. The two remaining parts were PART II: TASKS AND SCHEDULE and PART III: FINANCES. The content of PART II was later developed by staff, and the section on Finance was developed primarily by a Special Committee on Revenue appointed by the Authority Advisory Council. Each part of the plan was developed cooperatively by the AAC and staff, approved by the AAC, and then transmitted to the Board for adoption. The full plan was to be reviewed annually by the AAC.

The revised goals of CLASS as they appeared in Part I were:

1. To serve libraries so that they can provide better library service to users by:
   a. increasing library productivity and resources, and
   b. facilitating library resource sharing.
2. To achieve and maintain organizational and financial stability.

The Objectives, as delineated in Part I, were divided into two parts: Organizational Development and Technical Development.

J. MICHAEL BRUER: "On July 1, 1983, CLASS officially changed its name from the California Library Authority for Systems and Services to the Cooperative Library Agency for Systems and Services. The new name (which does not change the acronym) is a more accurate reflection of the nationwide orientation of CLASS.

CLASS was formed as an autonomous public agency that would act as the regional library network for the State of California. In the three years, 1980-83, the demand for CLASS's services from libraries outside California increased dramatically. With over five hundred members from coast to coast and thousands of customers, use of 'California' in the official name became anachronistic. In addition, CLASS has no jurisdictive responsibilities as the term 'Authority' suggests. The CLASS Board believed that the name change would help make the purpose of CLASS easier to interpret to the library community."

The three technical development objectives focused on (1) the integration of diverse automated systems, (2) development of message switching and teleprocessing capabilities, and (3) assistance to participants in the use of computer-based information systems and other innovations.

The "Implementation Emphases" section of Part I clustered CLASS activities into four groups: communication with the library community, statewide planning, technical development and assistance, and financial development. It should be noted especially that, within the cluster specifically relating to statewide planning, all segments of the CLASS membership unanimously asserted that CLASS would "coordinate joint planning and operational cooperation among libraries of all types" and "prepare, execute and maintain a Master Plan for library service throughout the state in cooperation and consultation with all segments and signatories, which is coordinated with segmental 'master plans' as well as with the CLASS five year plan."

With the elements of a long-range plan firmly in place, the CLASS Board met in March 1981 to assess the state of CLASS and decide how to resolve several complicated issues. These issues, raised by the Authority Advisory Council or by staff, induced the Board to:

1. Assess the strengths, weaknesses and progress of CLASS since June 1976, and develop ways to improve its effectiveness.
2. Decide if a presentation about CLASS progress should be made by the Board to the Signatories of the Joint Powers Agreement which formed CLASS.
3. Address the issue of stabilizing CLASS's financial base through legislative action, foundation development and/or conscientiously expanding its membership base and market area beyond California.
4. Evaluate policies and procedures for developing programs, products and services.

With the exception of topic 2, various committees of the membership and the Authority Advisory Council provided input on most of these issues, but firm decisions had not been made on most of them because their complexity and implications had not been fully explored.

During its March meeting, the CLASS Board unanimously approved a policy to guide the future development of CLASS. The policy focused on five aspects of the organization: cooperative services, development of new services, the relationship of the Board to the Authority Advisory Council, membership expansion, and reporting.

This policy resulted from discussions about several complex and intractable issues with which the organization had been wrestling for some time. Some of these issues were: (1) membership—fees, types, nationwide recruitment, services and the like; (2) the accountability of the AAC committees and task groups; (3) financing and cost recovery; (4) long and short range planning; (5) the relationship of CLASS to its segments as well as to other organizations; and (6) the possibility of state legislative support for CLASS.

After reviewing input and recommendations from members and staff, the Board concluded that much of the confusion and uncertainty about CLASS might be resolved if a relatively simple answer to a key question could be developed. That question was: "What is the business of CLASS?" Various purposes and "business areas" were isolated, discussed and rejected. Finally, the following policy emerged.

1. CLASS is, and should be seen as, a cooperative library service agency; that is, the main purpose of CLASS is to provide cooperative library services.
2. The cooperative library services provided should be those which can be provided more economically or more effectively through CLASS than by its individual members.
3. The cooperative library services offered should be those for which there is a reasonable expectation that cost can be recovered from some source.
4. A portion of the CLASS budget and activities should be devoted to exploration and development of new library services.
5. In regard to relationships between the Authority Advisory Council and the Board of Directors, the AAC should recommend desirable programs and services, and the Board should review the recommendations for financial feasibility, legality, and appropriateness to the organization, in light of the stated goals of the organization.
6. CLASS should pursue expansion of membership and services to other states and regions to the extent that cooperative library

services can be provided more economically and more effectively by doing so.
7. The Executive Director should report regularly to the Board on the status of development of present and proposed cooperative library services.

By asserting that CLASS is primarily a "cooperative library service agency," the Board affirmed that most of the staff's efforts should be devoted toward improving present services and developing new ones, rather than expending energy on other activities. Therefore, legislative activities, development of endowment fund support and constructing a new library foundation were activities which would not be undertaken, although they had been considered at various times in the past. Emphasis on cooperative services meant that instead of staff pressing for intersegmental planning and coordination, the segments and the membership must decide which products and services they want developed within the cooperative and mutually supportive environment which CLASS provided.

The Board invited review and comment on this policy by the Authority Advisory Council, the membership's representative body. The policy was seen as an instrument which sets direction; the details of implementation decisions would be dealt with as they arose.

In that same year, 1981, the consulting firm of Peat, Marwick, Mitchell and Company (PMM) was hired to conduct a management study of CLASS. In December 1981 they produced a report entitled "CLASS: A Study of the Organization, Management and Financial Plan" which recommended, among other things, that CLASS "modify the JEPA in order to streamline governance." In response, the Board appointed a Committee on Organization Streamlining (COOS), whose report was reviewed at length by the AAC and the Board, and was approved in the following form:

1. The Congress of Members should be eliminated.
2. The Authority Advisory Council should be eliminated.
3. The Board of Directors should be enlarged to include its present six voting members, plus nine non-voting members, allocated on the basis of general percentage of membership. (The Board at that time consisted of six voting members, two non-voting members, and the Chair of the AAC who voted in case of a tie.)

The Board asked the COOS to complete its analysis of the JEPA, seek legal counsel on modifying the document, modify the bylaws accordingly, and recommend an effective date for implementing the organizational change.

Another recommendation of the PMM management study was that the Board should survey the signatories of the Joint Powers Agreement which established CLASS to determine if those parties continue to support CLASS as an instrument for carrying out their objectives. The survey was eventually completed, and Board Chairman Steve Salmon reported that all signatories reaffirmed their support and use of CLASS; in addition, the non-voting segments of the Board also expressed their continuing support of the organization.

PMM recommended, and the Board agreed, that CLASS should focus on strengthening sales of existing products and services rather than developing new ones or expanding into new geographic markets where expertise may be minimal and financial risks high. The Board also requested that staff revise the current pricing policy, emphasizing advantages to members, and requested that the AAC revise the present membership fee structure.

In June, 1982, the COOS issued its recommendations for simplifying the governance structure of CLASS. These were reviewed by the AAC, which passed its comments and suggested changes on to the Board. The Board reviewed both the COOS' and the AAC's recommendations, made some changes of its own, and took action to implement the following:

1. Eliminate the Congress of Members,
2. Eliminate the Authority Advisory Council,
3. Enlarge the Board of Directors from six to fifteen.

Although the Congress of Members was eliminated as a body which holds annual meetings, member representatives would biennially elect non-voting Board representatives for their library segment. In other words, they would participate more directly in the governing process.

Likewise, although the Authority Advisory Council would be eliminated as a body which held regular meetings and appointed committees, there would be an opportunity for greater membership representation and more direct influence on the Board.

The fact that member representatives from the private sector were proposed as non-voting members of the Board was not seen as a problem. CLASS was formed under a Joint Powers Agreement which allowed only the public agency signatories to that document to be voting members. While the new organization was not viewed as ideal, Board members representing special and private academic libraries in past years indicated that they felt their non-voting status did not decrease their influence on Board decisions.

The Board was thus increased to fifteen members of which six retained voting privileges. The remaining nine members were apportioned to each of the segments according to aggregate membership size. Reapportionment would occur every two years. The governing principle behind this reorganization was the realization that the CLASS Board and membership are primarily interested in providing needed products and services to libraries. By decreasing the number of meetings, committees, and channels of approval necessary under the old governance structure, the organization would be better able to direct more energy and resources to improve library cooperation and effectiveness.

By January 1983, CLASS membership stood at 539 libraries throughout North America, as well as several thousand other libraries that utilize one or more CLASS services on a non-member basis. The annual membership renewal campaign which began in May 1983 reminded both members and potential members of the many benefits of membership in the organization.

CLASS, acting as a buying cooperative on behalf of the membership, maintains special contractual arrangements with DIALOG, BRS, and other vendors through which many members earn substantial discounts, in some cases saving thousands of dollars each year in connect charges.

CLASS provides cost-effective access to a variety of computer-based services such as RLIN shared cataloging and acquisitions, the Ontyme electronic mail system, and microcomputer-based software for library applications.

Other immediate financial benefits of CLASS membership are the discounts on library supplies and furniture available from Brodart, University Products and Demco. CLASS members receive discounts on the California Union List of Periodicals, the California Academic Libraries List of Serials, the California Data Base for Monographs and other publications. Microcomputer and other equipment discounts are also available.

Perhaps even more significantly, CLASS members participate in the development of new products and services. Membership in

CLASS is an opportunity to support cooperation and resource sharing. In many diverse groups, CLASS consists of libraries working together to create the future and provide better and more cost-effective services to the library user.

With this all-too-brief recapitulation of the background and history of CLASS, I would like to return to a couple of points I made at the beginning when I called attention to lessons learned as a consequence of the CLASS experiment in networking. From the foregoing exposition it should be clear that there is an interrelationship between the issue of governance and the issue of organizational behavior and product or service development. Librarians quite correctly value cooperation and resource sharing as means to serve their users better. But sometimes the framework erected to accomplish the avowed objectives can be so cumbersome as to obscure the goals and impede the actions necessary to achieve those ends. There is no question but that cooperation implies participation, but it is, after all, the results of cooperation that count for more than the methodology.

Recognizing this, the leadership of CLASS took steps to streamline the organization and to simplify the governance structure. The result was a substantial reduction in the number of people involved with decision making outside of the staff. There was clear recognition of the fact that an organization with limited resources must run lean if it is to run at all. It was also recognized that, if CLASS were to make good on the requirement that it be self-supporting, the cost of overhead was a significant limiting factor and must therefore be reduced as much as possible.

At the same time, efforts were made to clarify the mission of the organization, perhaps a matter of even greater importance than that of governance structure. There can be little doubt that, if those who start an enterprise do not know *exactly* what they are trying to do, they will experience considerable difficulty no matter *how* they go about it. The goals of CLASS as expressed in the 1976 JEPA were rather imprecise, as were the conflicting expectations of the major participants, although they have for the most part gone largely unrecorded. The Board was therefore right on target when, in 1981, it sought to answer the question: "What is the business of CLASS?" Indeed, this is a question which any enterprise would do well to ask itself periodically, if only to be reassured that its behavior is still in tune with its objectives. In this way, CLASS was able to conclude that it was in the business of providing cooperative library services.

This leads to the question of what is meant by cooperation and how it relates to the future of CLASS and of networking in general. The OED defines cooperation as "the action of working together towards the same end, purpose, or effect," and is therefore of little help in this instance since it begs the question of substituting the phrase "working together." The term "library cooperation" has become almost hackneyed because of imprecise application and casual overuse. There are many examples, on the local level at least, of groups of libraries working together toward a common end, but it often comes down to everybody agreeing to "cooperate" so long as it is to their own advantage. True cooperation, it seems to me, must mean that at least part of the time, some of the participants are willing to sacrifice short-term advantages for the sake of a greater purpose. This hardly ever happens, and it is often convenient to fall back on higher authority, such as the "University" or "Town Council," to explain why a given contribution can not be made.

It may perhaps be argued that I am overly critical of library cooperation as it has evidenced itself at the local level, and that may very well be true. But there is no question whatever in my mind that networks, representing at least in theory the epitome of cooperative library organizations, are becoming more and more competitive rather than cooperative. It if be granted that groups of local libraries have demonstrated substantial progress over the years in working out cooperative relationships, the problem seems to have simply moved up one level. Networks openly compete to provide services rather than cooperate for the benefit of the end user and their constituent members. It would not be unfair to suggest that cooperation is sometimes used as a tool in the service of competition; that is to say, movements toward apparent cooperation may be nothing more than thinly disguised efforts to find a new market, or to learn who is doing what, or to undercut the competition, or to ensure that a given market does not have to be shared with anyone else. The problem can be expressed less pejoratively by suggesting that networks are using cooperation as a marketing tool in an attempt to attract more customers, if you will, to their brand of cooperation. But in either case it can scarcely be called library cooperation in any traditional sense of the term.

When faced with obvious opportunities to cooperate, networks have also been known to cite external, authoritarian reasons for not doing so by saying, for example, "it is not in our standard contract," or "it wouldn't have our name on it." Similarly, the old "not in-

J. MICHAEL BRUER: "It may perhaps be argued that I am overly critical of library cooperation as it has evidenced itself at the local level, and that may very well be true. But there is no question whatever in my mind that networks, representing at least in theory the epitome of cooperative library organizations, are becoming more and more competitive rather than cooperative. . . . Networks openly compete to provide services rather than cooperate for the benefit of the end user and their constituent members."

vented here'' syndrome, once so rampant in the field of library automation, has greatly impeded the growth of network cooperation. A few observers have even detected incipient signs of creeping monopolism and a sort of professional chutzpah: what's good for our network is good for the world.

Having said all that, it is possible that the issue of network cooperation versus competition is a non-problem in that the very nature of networks, insofar as they relate to each other, may be essentially a competitive one. To a degree, networks are already seen as vendors rather than as member-based cooperatives, even by their own members. Not to put too fine a point on it, if networking is a business rather than an eleemosynary endeavor, then competition is the name of the game, and cooperation is akin to collusion. It may be that networks on the regional or national level can function only in a competitive environment. Or perhaps library cooperation on a large scale is just too expensive *not* to be treated as a business, which is another way of saying that there is no free lunch when the traditional bartering of services breaks down. In any case, this is an issue which I believe should be explicitly resolved, for etymological, practical and professional reasons.

Unfortunately, if networks continue to develop as competitive business enterprises, as they give every indication of doing, it may be increasingly difficult to find people within the library profession who are equipped to function in that environment. Good network librarians are hard to find even today, as anyone who is experienced with network staff development will attest. Often the initial excitement shown by promising recruits to the network environment is later tempered by disillusionment. It is rarely an entrepreneurial spirit that attracts people to library school, and the curricula even more rarely train the students in sales techniques, marketing skills, business planning, and the other paraphernalia collecting around network management these days.

I have raised these issues of competition versus cooperation and entrepreneurialism versus professionalism not to cast a pall on our proceedings, but to make explicit certain aspects of network development which might otherwise come to eventual fruition more or less by accident. There may be no reason why library networks should not function as competitive business enterprises, and be directed and managed by non-librarians, but it would be better, in my view, if the profession were to examine these issues and come to its own conclusions, rather than have them imposed by fiat or default.

J. MICHAEL BRUER: "To a degree, networks are already seen as vendors rather than as member-based cooperatives, even by their own members. Not to put too fine a point on it, if networking is a business rather than an eleemosynary endeavor, then competition is the name of the game, and cooperation is akin to collusion."

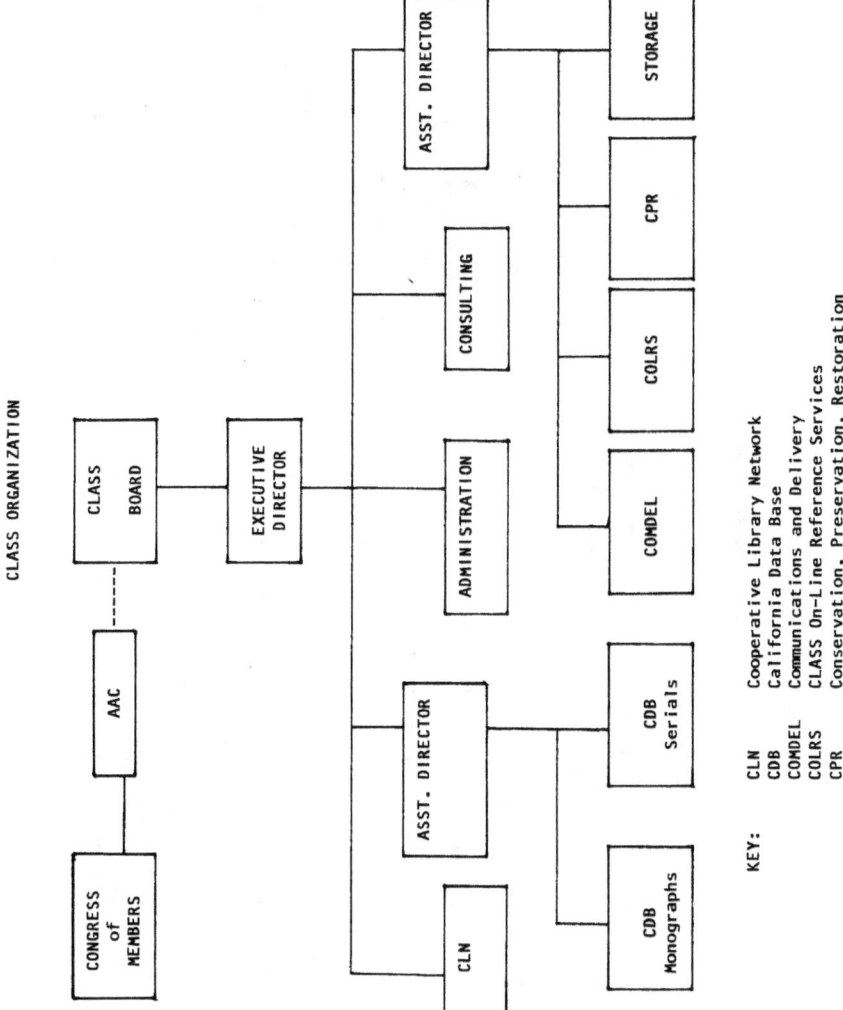

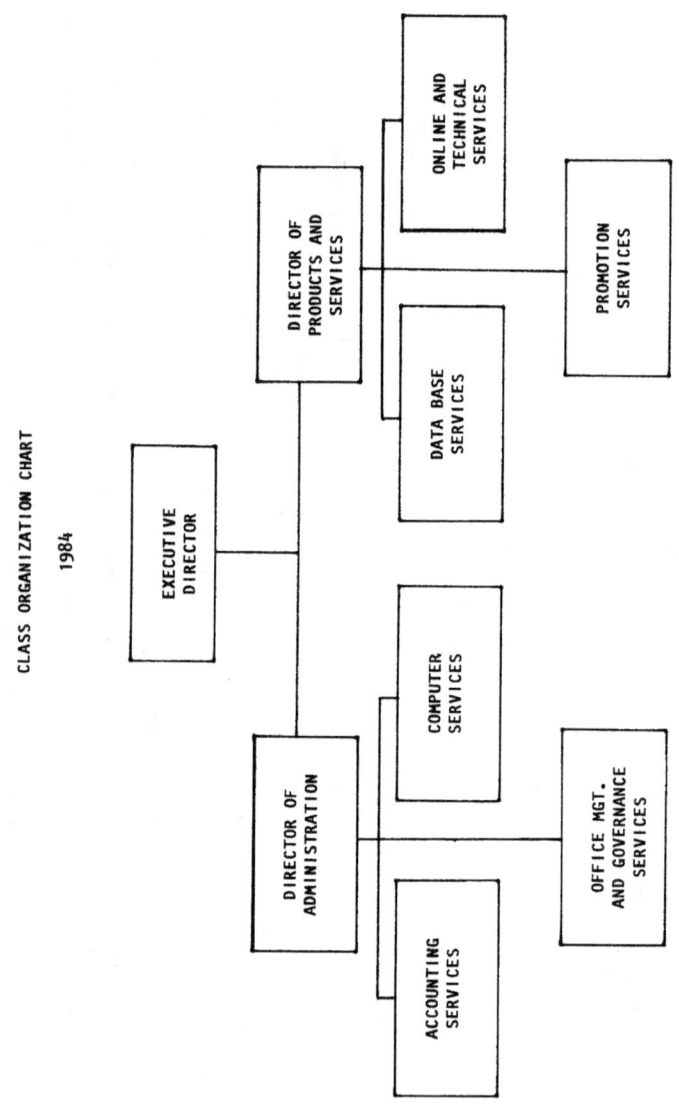

Someone once said that the prime purpose of eloquence is to keep other people from speaking—an objective which I believe I have attained over the last several minutes—although I hasten to reject any claim to eloquence in the process. I am, at the same time, struck with the realization that nowhere in my exposition have I used the term "books," even here in the august company of fellow librarians. Nor can I recollect any of the previous speakers having referred to the subject of books, even in passing. This is an oversight which we can not let pass unnoticed and unrectified. Perhaps I can save the day by calling your attention to Ring Lardner, whose remark about the subject of books seemed to cover it all when he said: "(My friend) took me into his library and showed me his books, of which he has a complete set." With that, I think there is little more to be said, and I thank you for your attention.

* * *

Bridget Lamont

Thank you, Michael. I have a lot of notes. Briefly, we're going to break for lunch and then we'll have lunch. Then we'll return to hear Fred Kilgour and Al Trezza. I hope we'll be hearing more about the role of networks in marketing, why people really join networks, if we would have had networks or be talking about them the same way without mentioning OCLC, the role of personalities and environments in dictating network structures (I liked Alice's comment of "formerly independent libraries" who joined networks), whether or not library networks *are* becoming more competitive, and whether or not library networks can function only on that competitive basis. Those are only a few things that I hope we'll hear more about this afternoon and I'm sure you have some things as well.

We'll have lunch now, thank you.

AFTERNOON SESSION

Experience and Expectation

Frederick G. Kilgour

Founder Trustee
OCLC, Inc.
Dublin, Ohio

(Introductory Remarks by Bridget Lamont)

Those of you who've finished eating, I think have had time to move around. I've seen some people with their Marshall Fields' shopping bags. I know some people got a little fresh air at lunch and I think we're ready to get on with this afternoon's presentations.

It's my privilege to introduce the next speaker, Frederick Kilgour, *the* Founder Trustee of OCLC. It's difficult for me to prepare introductory remarks about Mr. Kilgour, but I might say that he started as President and Executive Director of OCLC, worked his way up as Vice Chairman of the Board of Trustees, and now he's known as the Founder Trustee on the Board of Directors. In addition, he served as Professor of Library Administration at Ohio State University, handled a variety of functions at Yale University, and his list of activities and his vitae is, at the very least, most impressive. He's been a Librarian of the Year. He's received the Margaret Mann Citation from the American Library Association, the Melvill Dewey Award, and on, and on, and on. I think—I hope Mr. Kilgour will be talking about whether or not there really was library networking before OCLC, but when I asked some of my Illinois colleagues a few minutes ago, "What can I say to introduce this gentleman?" they said, "Well just point out that now that everybody else has had their shots at OCLC this is a good time for him to stand up and talk."

Mr. Kilgour.

* * *

Bridget, I can assure you this isn't the first time [everybody has had their shots at OCLC].

Find the right talk . . . here we are. I was wandering through a splendid one on microcomputers that might interest you, but I finally found one entitled "Experience and Expectation."

INTRODUCTION

This talk is about my experience and expectations with respect to computerized networks, and I will begin by recollecting snatches from my experiences that might be termed pre-history of OCLC, selecting particular episodes from which there are lessons to learn. Some of those lessons teach us that a flawed means of achieving something can be better than no achievement at all.

The pre-history to which I refer was the development, organization, and operation of the U.S. Government's Interdepartmental Committee for the Acquisition of Foreign Publications (IDC) during World War II, of which I was Acting Chairman and chief executive during most of its existence. The Committee was composed of a dozen government agencies and its function was to obtain publications from enemy and enemy occupied areas for intelligence purposes. IDC had seven positions and a staff of three when I joined it in March 1942; a year and a half later the staff numbered 150 with 90 in Washington and 60 overseas.[1] Like OCLC, IDC worked.

From the Autumn of 1942 until the end of the war I was Acting Chairman by default. Organizationally IDC was located in the Office of Strategic Services (OSS) and its first and only chairman was an OSS official. Because the Committee members placed such high value on intelligence in foreign publications and because they greatly feared that OSS would receive preference over other agencies in receipt of that intelligence, they forced the resignation of that first chairman. It immediately developed that a chairman from any agency was going to be suspect of obtaining preference, so it fell upon me to be Acting Chairman, for which capacity I adopted a policy of strict neutrality and constant communication. I literally became a professional luncher, and few days passed when I did not lunch with one or more of the influential members of the Committee.

The conceptual pre-history of OCLC lies in the Columbia-Harvard-Yale (CHY) Medical Libraries Computerization Project;[2] the benefits of the small online CHY network were to be reduced costs of cataloging, and computerized information retrieval. The project got underway late in 1961 at Yale where I was Medical Librarian, and its development immediately accelerated when the National Science Foundation (NSF) awarded it a grant in 1963. Unfortunately CHY collapsed in 1965 when Harvard withdrew. Had one of the most influential agencies in IDC withdrawn there might have been considerable rocking of the boat, but it would not have sunk; the withdrawal of one participant from CHY promptly scuttled the Project.

IDC with a dozen members but only one source of funds was a stable organization. Had each member of so few provided funds individually, the departure or threat of departure of one or two would have rocked, or perhaps sunk, the boat. Because it had only three participants CHY, even with assured single source of financing, was scuttled when Harvard withdrew.

OCLC—RETROSPECTION

When I joined OCLC in August 1967 as Executive Director and first staff member, membership in OCLC comprised 54 Ohio colleges and universities and paying assessments, so that although four members had departed from the fold by August 1971 when OCLC initiated online operation the organization remained stable and still had sufficient funds to operate.

Problems

No sooner had online operations started than libraries outside Ohio began to request participation. The Ohio membership in an expression of regionalism would not approve operation outside Ohio except for extending the network into Pittsburgh in neighboring Pennsylvania so that the OCLC network would enjoy interstate long distance telephone charges instead of the much more expensive intrastate charges. The Ohio Membership had several reasons for resisting expansion, not the least of which was that they had furnished $300,000 of the $405,000 that had been expended to invent, develop, and implement the online system. Curiously enough, lack of capital was not one of the reasons put forth; actually had OCLC attempted to expand outside Ohio in late 1971 or in 1972, it could not have done so without risking bankruptcy from the under-capitalization that would immediately have been induced.

A compromise involved three-year agreements with several library networks already in existence and with new networks incorporated for the prime purpose of signing agreements with OCLC. Because of Ohio's regionalistic position it was intended that these networks would replicate the OCLC system and be operating independently by the end of the three years. Such was not to be, for lack of capital and human resources made replications infeasible. So there came into being the awkward system of independent regional networks using the OCLC system that has plagued OCLC, the networks, and participating libraries ever since.

Curiously enough, each new network immediately took the former position of the Ohio Membership as soon as it joined the OCLC system and resisted any further extension of OCLC operations. This attitude persists today, for there are librarians, I think, who should know better by now, who are protesting OCLC's extension internationally.

I had long had the professional goal of participating in bringing a nationwide online computerized network of libraries into being, but as long as the Ohio Membership held the position that each regional network should either replicate the OCLC online system or invent, develop, and implement its own system, it was clear to me that there was no way in which a group of independent regions could be integrated into a nationwide system. There were a variety of obstacles besides regionalism: intense difficulties in planning, organization, coordination, and operation. I therefore responded affirmatively late in 1973 when another not-for-profit organization operating nationally invited me to accept a position to develop a nationwide computerization of libraries under its aegis. My wife and I had twice visited the new area to look for housing before I had an opportunity to apprise the OCLC trustees of my intention. To my surprise, when I did inform them, they immediately reversed their position under the leadership of one of the state university presidents. On 21 May

1974 a meeting of the Ohio Membership amended the purpose clause of the Articles of Incorporation to state clearly that OCLC is empowered to operate a national network as well as an international network. I stayed on, but the damage had been done. No one in his right mind would organize a nationwide online computerized library network made up of independent regional networks on the OCLC model. RLG, UTLAS, and WLN are organized rationally, none of the other eight online computerized library networks in the world use the OCLC model, with the partial exception of that in West Germany, if indeed the latter ever comes into being.

The Ohio Membership retained governance within Ohio in the Spring of 1974 when it extended its operations nationally and internationally. This retention of governance was done on the basis of "who else knows how to do it" with a considerable amount of justification although I told the Membership at that time that it would be impossible for Ohio to continue for long to govern a nationwide network. Quite properly, institutions outside of Ohio soon demanded to participate in governance. I well remember a meeting in New England when the demands became attacks with the most prominent phrase flung at me on the podium being "taxation without representation." The mounting intensity of dissatisfaction forced establishment of a new governance, which came into being in December 1977. The condition that everyone knew but some did not accept, namely that you cannot have a membership organization governed in its entirety by only one regional group, was finally accepted by all.

In spite of governance problems OCLC worked from the beginning, and today is run in a business-like manner as any large for-profit or not-for-profit corporation. OCLC continues to fulfill its original goals, which were to increase availability of library materials to users of libraries, and to decrease rate of rise of per-unit costs that were threatening to undermine libraries, as well as continuing to further its expressed purpose of promoting evolution of the use of libraries, of libraries themselves, and of librarianship.

What were the aspects of the OCLC network that contributed to its success? As I have already stated, the membership was large enough for stability and provided sufficient funds for initial development. On the other hand it was small enough to be governable and it was homogeneous, being originally composed only of Ohio colleges and universities having common goals and a history of cooperation.

Although at first not seemingly of sufficient importance to attract

FREDERICK G. KILGOUR: "I had long had the professional goal of participating in bringing a nationwide online computerized network of libraries into being, but as long as the Ohio Membership held the position that each regional network should either replicate the OCLC online system or invent, develop, and implement its own systems, it was clear to me that there was no way in which a group of independent regions could be integrated into a nationwide system. . . . I therefore responded affirmatively late in 1973 when another not-for-profit organization operating nationally invited me to accept a position to develop a nationwide computerization of libraries under its aegis."

large grants for development (only $105,000 in grants was expended), OCLC had enough time and capital for careful design of a true network rather than extension of computerization of a single library to serve several. There was time for research and development of derived, truncated search keys designed for library users as well as librarians, simulation studies to identify efficient hardware, and testing of programs on a small and modular scale, all of great importance in a pioneer enterprise. The network attracted young and venturesome engineers and stimulated librarians who were willing to contribute to the doing of new things in new ways.

Finally, revenues, capitalization, and staffing growth were able to keep pace with the demands of geographic expansion as well as extension to all types of libraries.

Successful Goal Achievement

OCLC has also greatly increased availability of library resources with its inexpensive and first-to-be-produced online union catalog.[3] It was possible to demonstrate after the first half-dozen years of activity that resources in small libraries were being made far more available than had been the case prior to their participation in OCLC, and that these smaller libraries were slowing the rate of rise of interlibrary loan requests addressed to large libraries.[4] As for absolute increase in availability of library materials, the OCLC system processed online interlibrary loan requests among libraries during February 1984 at an annual rate of over two million requests.

OCLC has also been successful in attaining the second of its two primary goals, reducing rate of rise of per-unit costs in libraries particularly by increasing productivity of cataloging staffs. Statistical validation of this statement is not easy to produce largely because of the absence of statistics prior to online computerization, but it has been shown that productivity in academic libraries can be increased from one-quarter to two-fifths.[5] These increases in productivity were made possible by economies of scale that a large, centralized network can provide for individual libraries. These economies of scale take the form of huge amounts of computer power that individual libraries could not afford for themselves, and enormous quantities of available cataloging information that would be equally unaffordable.

The most exciting advance that online computerized networks have introduced is the imaginative capability of doing new things in

FREDERICK G. KILGOUR: "... the OCLC system does a variety of new things in new ways, one example of which is the miniature catalog concept.[6] This new concept is entirely nonexistent in traditional librarianship, and has yet to make its major contribution to libraries and their users. This contribution will come when local libraries have their own online catalogs consisting of myriads of miniature catalogs."

new ways. The vast majority of computer applications comprise doing old things in new ways, and, indeed, institutions use OCLC for the most part to do old things in new ways. However, the OCLC system does a variety of new things in new ways, one example of which is the miniature catalog concept.[6] This new concept is entirely nonexistent in traditional librarianship, and has yet to make its major contribution to libraries and their users. This contribution will come when local libraries have their own online catalogs consisting of myriads of miniature catalogs. The average number of entries in these miniature catalogs will rarely exceed three, and when librarianship recognizes that its catalogs have only an average of three or fewer entries there will be enormous simplification in the production of catalogs.[7] It certainly will be no longer necessary to have to use five hundred pages of cataloging rules as in the second edition of *Anglo-American Cataloging Rules*.

EXPECTATION

Proliferation of new high technology in the early 1980s is bringing about an extensive evolution of the networks of the 1970s. The major current event altering the character of the online networks of the 1970s is the migration of computer power in small but affordable amounts not only into libraries, but also into homes, workplaces, and schools. This migration has the effect of diminishing the economies of scale enjoyed from central sites in the last decade, but it does not eliminate these economies nor does it have a significant effect at least in the immediate future, on the economy of scale of storing amounts of cataloging information centrally.

The migration of computer power into homes, workplaces including libraries, and academe presents a marvelous opportunity for computerized networks to increase availability of information to users of information. The principal challenge presented is that of doing new things in new ways. Coincidental with the rising torrent of microcomputers is the increasing availability of published materials in digital form. In addition the next couple of decades hold the prospect of digitized telephony, which will greatly facilitate microcomputers being employed as communication devices, and digitized television, which together with digitized telephony will convert television sets into readily usable information terminals.

These events will make possible provision of information to users

FREDERICK G. KILGOUR: "Coincidental with the rising torrent of microcomputers is the increasing availability of published materials in digital form. In addition the next couple of decades hold the prospect of digitized telephony, which will greatly facilitate the microcomputers being employed as communication devices, and digitized television, which together with digitized telephony will convert television sets into readily usable information terminals."

when and where they need it by information systems such as the OCLC Content Retrieval System (OCRS) currently in the invention/ development phase. In brief, it is anticipated that OCRS will sell to libraries catalog information together with contents page and index information that will be available to microcomputers and other terminals in the community. A central site such as a computerized network or publisher will house the digital text of a book, which users will access with brief response time to enable them to browse the text to obtain data desired. Such a system certainly meets the challenge of doing new things in new ways.

SUMMARY

Experience reported in this paper directs attention to the fact that a group of institutions working together cooperatively is unstable if one or several of the institutions can effect its demise by withdrawal. It is also made clear that the unique regional network organization like that of the intermediaries marketing and servicing OCLC processes and products can be made to work, even if at a toll to the libraries, regional networks, and the central computerized network that supplies the processes and products.

More positively computers can be used to do new things in new ways to increase availability of information to those needing it and can do so when and where they need it. At the same time computerized networks can reduce the rate of rise of per-unit costs in institutions serving information users.

REFERENCES

1. Richards, Pamela Spence. "Gathering Enemy Scientific Information in Wartime: The OSS and the Periodical Republication Program." *Journal of Library History* 16 (1981):253-64.

2. Kilgour, Frederick G. "Basic Systems Assumptions of the Columbia-Harvard-Yale Medical Libraries Computerization Project." In *Collected Papers of Frederick G. Kilgour: Early Years.* Dublin, Ohio: OCLC Online Computer Library Center, Inc., 1984. 309-314. (First published in Institute on Information Retrieval (2d:1965.)) *Information Retrieval With Special Reference to the Biomedical Sciences.* Minneapolis: University of Minnesota, 1966. 145-54.

3. Kilgour, Frederick G. "Online Union Catalogs: Revolutionary in Function and Design." (In press.)

4. Kilgour, Frederick G. "Interlibrary Loans Online." In *Collected Papers of Frederick G. Kilgour: OCLC Years.* Dublin, Ohio: OCLC Online Computer Library Center, Inc., 1984. 405-409. (First published in *Library Journal* 104:1979, 460-63.)

5. Kilgour, Frederick G. "Increased Productivity of Catalog Production in a Computerized Network." In *Ibid.* 491-94. (First published in *Increasing Productivity through Library Automation: Essen Symposium, 11 October - 14 October 1982.*) Essen: Gesamthochschulbibliothek, 1983. 101-112.

6. Kilgour, Frederick G. "Library Catalog Design." In *Ibid.* 473-76. (First published in *5th International Online Meeting, London, 8-10 December 1981.*) Oxford, England: Learned Information. 1981. 169-73.

7. Kilgour, Frederick G. "The Online Catalog Revolution." *Library Journal* 109:1984, 319-21. (First published in *New Trends in Electronic Publishing and Electronic Libraries: Essen Symposium, 29 August-31 August 1983.*) Essen: Gesamthochschulbibliothek, 1984. 73-87.

The National Commission on Libraries and Information Sciences: Past Accomplishments—Future Prospects

Alphonse F. Trezza

Associate Professor
School of Library and Information Studies
The Florida State University
Tallahassee, Florida

(Introductory Remarks by Bridget Lamont)

Our next speaker is the former Executive Director for the National Commission on Libraries and Information Services. He's been President of the Continuing Library Education Network and Exchange, very active in numerous American Library Association activities and his background goes on, and on, and on. Currently, among a variety of other things, Al is working on new standards for public libraries in Florida. He has contributed a great deal to library cooperation and library networking. I hope that he'll make some comments from the perspective of a library educator today on the future for potential for training new experts, or new entrepreneurs (whatever you'll call them) in the area of library networking. It's really a privilege for me to introduce my mentor in library cooperation and networking, Al Trezza.

Welcome back to Illinois!

* * *

It's always nice to be back in Illinois. I must tell you, Bridget was a wonderful student; you can see the results by where she is today. There were a couple of comments earlier about pin-stripe suits, and I can't let it pass without saying that I've been wearing mine because my wife packed it, and I dress the way my wife packs it.

The National Commission on Libraries and Information Science is the only organization we're going to be talking about today which is a non-operating agency. All the others are called "operating agencies," and the Commission is not. The Commission, by law, is not an operating agency.

The first part of my presentation will consist of a review of the past. It will include a discussion of the historical beginnings of the National Commission on Libraries and Information Sciences. I will then trace the activities from 1970 to 1979. After that I will give some reflections on my tenure with NCLIS and finally, I will give my feelings and suggestions for the next fifteen years.

The idea for a national commission on libraries developed in the early sixties. Many diverse groups such as the American Library Association, the U.S. Bureau of the Budget (now the Office of Management and Budget), the Office of Science and Technology, the U.S. Office of Education and the American Council of Learned Societies were interested in such a development.

There was active support of the idea during the Kennedy Administration. The establishment of a commission was delayed as a result of the tragic death of President Kennedy. In the fall of 1966, President Johnson established, by Executive Order, a National Commission on Libraries. The temporary commission was charged with four responsibilities:

1. Make a comprehensive study and appraisal of the role of libraries as resources for scholarly pursuits, as centers for the dissemination of knowledge, and as components of the evolving national information systems;
2. Appraise the policies, programs, and practices of public agencies and private institutions and organizations together with other factors which have a bearing on the role and effective utilization of libraries;
3. Appraise library funding, including Federal support of libraries, to determine how funds available for the construction and support of libraries and library services can be more effectively and efficiently utilized; and
4. Develop recommendations for action by Government or private institutions and organizations designed to ensure an effective and efficient library system for the nation.

ALPHONSE F. TREZZA: "The idea for a national commission on libraries developed in the early sixties. . . . There was active support of the idea during the Kennedy Administration. The establishment of a commission was delayed as a result of the tragic death of President Kennedy. In the fall of 1966, President Johnson established, by Executive Order, a National Commission on Libraries. . . . The Commission of twenty librarians and educators was headed by a distinguished team . . . Its fundamental recommendation was, 'That it be declared National Policy, enunciated by the President and enacted into law by the Congress, that the American people should be provided with library and information services adequate to their needs, and that the Federal Government, in collaboration with the state and local governments and private agencies, should exercise leadership in assuring the provision of such services.' ''

The Commission of twenty librarians and educators was headed by a distinguished team—Douglas M. Knight, President of Duke University, Chairman, and Frederick Burkhardt, President of the American Council of Learned Societies, Vice-Chairman. The Commission met eleven times, held many regional hearings, sponsored thirteen special studies and on July 1, 1968, issued its report and recommendations. Its fundamental recommendation was, "That it be declared National Policy, enunciated by the President and enacted into law by the Congress, that the American people should be provided with library and information services adequate to their needs, and that the Federal Government, in collaboration with the state and local governments and private agencies, should exercise leadership in assuring the provision of such services."

To work toward the achievement of this goal, six broad and fundamental objectives were formulated and five specific recommendations designed to provide a sound basis for a realistic means for immediate action were enunciated.

The recommendations were as follows:

1. The establishment of a National Commission on Libraries and Information Science as a continuing Federal planning agency.
2. The recognition and strengthening of the role of the Library of Congress as the National Library of the United States and establishment of a Board of Advisers.
3. The establishment of a Federal Institute of Library and Information Science as a principal center for basic and applied research in all relevant areas.
4. The recognition and full acceptance of the critically important role the United States Office of Education currently plays in meeting needs for library services.
5. The strengthening of state library agencies to overcome deficiencies in fulfilling their current functions.

To implement the first recommendation, bills were presented to the 91st Congress (1969) and hearings were held in the spring. Members of Congress, former members of the Advisory Commission, the Librarian of Congress, and leaders of library and educational organizations gave their enthusiastic support to the proposed legislation. The only dissenting voice was from an official of the Office of Education. He contended that the proposed Commission should not be an independent agency, that several of its members should be high governmental officials, and that all of the appointed members should be named by the Secretary of Health, Education, and Welfare. The Congress responded by passing the bill establishing a National Commission on Libraries and Information Science as a permanent, independent agency with a membership consisting of:

> The Librarian of Congress and fourteen members appointed by the President, by and with the advice and consent of the Senate. Five members of the Commission shall be professional librarians or information specialists, and the remainder shall be persons having special competence or interest in the needs of our society for library and information services, at least one of whom shall be knowledgeable with respect to the technological aspects of library and information service and science needs of the elderly. One of the members of the Commission shall be designated by the President as chairman of the Commission. The terms of office of the appointive members of the Commission shall be five years.

The bill was signed into law (Public Law 91-345) on July 20, 1970, and the first Commission members were appointed in July 1971. The Commission held its first meeting in September of that year. The importance and impact for libraries and information services of this law cannot be overstated. The law provides a strong, positive national policy:

> The Congress hereby affirms that library and information services adequate to achieve national goals and to utilize most effectively the Nation's educational resources and that the Federal Government will cooperate with State and local governments and public and private agencies in assuring optimum provision of such services.

The law assigns to the Commission primary responsibility for developing and recommending overall plans for meeting national library and informational needs and for advising the President and the Congress on implementation of national policy. The Commission has the responsibility for developing plans for the coordination of activities at the Federal, state and local levels; for advising Federal, state, local and private agencies regarding library and information science; for appraising the adequacies and deficiencies of current library and information resources and services, and for evaluating the effectiveness of current library and information science programs.

The Commission is authorized to conduct studies, surveys, and analyses of the library and information needs of the nation, including the special library and informational needs of rural areas, of economically, socially, or culturally deprived persons, and of elderly persons, and the means by which these needs may be met through information centers, through the libraries of elementary and secondary schools and institutions of higher education, and through public, research, special, and other types of libraries; and to promote research and development activities which will extend and improve the nation's library and information-handling capability as essential links in the national communications networks.

The Commission decided that its first step should be to develop a national program for library and information services to provide a framework and focus for its efforts. The Commission recognized that an effective program could only be developed with the active participation of the library and information science community.

The Commission held regional hearings through the United States. They were sited to give the widest possible geographic coverage, and they were organized, publicized and conducted so as to evoke the broadest possible demographic response. In addition to these formal hearings, various commissioners, singly and in small groups, conducted mini-hearings to delve more deeply into the problems of special constituencies and in 1973, the Commission sponsored a special two-day invitational conference on user needs. The Commission also endeavored to develop and maintain constant two-way communication with major associations and institutions.

The response to the initial versions of the program document was gratifying. In spite of initial distributions in the thousands of copies, the issuance of every draft and revision resulted in a flood of requests for copies. Suggestions for changes, additions, deletions et al., came to the Commission by postcards, letters, and formal statements; by written and oral testimony at hearings; and by telephone and telegram. Commissioners and staff were approached at meetings and conferences by individuals and groups of people who wanted to offer their comments. The volume of comment would have been, by itself, encouraging. However, the comments revealed that most people were reading the documents thoroughly and offering suggestions on the basis of careful analysis. For the most part, the criticisms were constructive in intent and focused on priorities

ALPHONSE F. TREZZA: "The Commission decided that its first step should be to develop a national program for library and information services to provide a framework and focus for its efforts. The Commission recognized that an effective program could only be developed with the active participation of the library and information science community. . . . .

The response to the initial versions of the program document was gratifying. In spite of initial distributions in the thousands of copies, the issuance of every draft and revision resulted in a flood of requests for copies. Suggestions for changes, additions, deletions et al., came to the Commission by postcards, letters, and formal statements; by written and oral testimony at hearings; and by telephone and telegram. Commissioners and staff were approached at meetings and conferences by individuals and groups of people who wanted to offer their comments."

and perceived emphases, without challenging the basic concepts and objectives.

It was, of course, impossible to incorporate all of the suggestions the Commission received into the program document. Every suggestion was considered in the preparation of the final document, which represented, as nearly as could be achieved, a consensus of the library/information community and the public at large on the assumptions and objectives of a national program.

The National Program Document, "Toward a National Program for Library and Information Service: Goals for Action," was adopted by the Commission in May 1975 and published in June. It quickly received the support, in principle and concept, of the major professional library and information service associations—The American Library Association, the Association of Research Libraries, the Special Libraries Association, the American Society for Information Science, the Medical Library Association, the American Association of Law Libraries, the Catholic Library Association, and the National Federation of Abstracting and Indexing Services.

The program document clearly reflected the Commission's working philosophy, which was user-oriented. It was the Commission's intent that the users of information, including potential as well as current users, should be the principal focus of a national program. Its overall goal was and still is:

> To eventually provide every individual in the United States with equal opportunity to access to that part of the total information resource which will satisfy the individual's educational, working, cultural and leisure-time needs and interests, regardless of the individual's location, social or physical condition or level of intellectual achievement.

The Commission identified in the program document five assumptions and eight objectives which were formulated on the basis of the testimony received through regional hearings and reflected a sense of national needs from user communities throughout the nation. The five basic assumptions are:

1. That the total library and information resource in the United States is a national resources which should be developed, strengthened, organized and made available to the maximum degree possible in the public interest. This national resource

represents the cumulated and growing record of much of our nation's, and indeed, much of the world's, total cultural experience—intellectual, social, technological, and spiritual.
2. That all of the people of the United States have the right, according to their individual needs, to realistic and convenient access to this national resource for their personal enrichment and achievement, and thereby for the progress of society.
3. That with the help of new technology and with national resolve, the disparate and discrete collections of recorded information in the United States can become, in due course, an integrated national network.
4. That the rights and interests of authors, publishers, and other providers of information be recognized in the national program in ways which maintain their economic and competitive viability.
5. That legislation devised for the coherent development of library and information services will not undermine constitutionally-protected rights of personal privacy and intellectual freedom, and will preserve local, state and regional autonomy.

The eight objectives are:

1. "To ensure that basic minimums of library and information services adequate to meet the needs of all local communities are satisfied."
2. "Provide adequate special services to special constituencies, including the unserved."
3. "Strengthen existing statewide resources and systems."
4. "Ensure basic and continuing education of personnel essential to the implementation of a national program."
5. "Coordinate existing Federal programs for library and information service."
6. "Encourage the private sector (comprising organizations which are not directly tax-supported) to become an active partner in the development of the national program."
7. "Establish a locus of Federal responsibility charged with implementing the national network and coordinating the national program under the policy guidance of the National Commission."
8. "Plan, develop, and implement a nationwide network of library and information service."

With the completion, publication and general acceptance of the National Program Document, the emphasis shifted from program development to implementation. The Commission decided not to attempt a revolutionary approach, i.e., a grand systems design and a call for large expenditures. Practical considerations dictated the choice of an evolutionary approach. The Commission reasoned that, even in the unlikely event that the money could be found, there simply was not enough information available upon which to base such a design. In the second place, technological, economic, and sociological changes were reaching exponential rates. By the time such a grand design could be developed, funded, executed and put in place, it would already be obsolete. Finally, such a grand design would certainly give the impression—if not the substance—of a massive, monolithic Federal presence in library and information services, which is antithetical to the political and philosophical underpinnings of the United States, and contrary to the expressed intent of the NCLIS to avoid any such authoritarian superstructure.

The evolutionary approach required a kind of double vision. While one eye was focused on what was achievable currently or in the immediate future, the other had to remain firmly fixed on the eight objectives to ensure that the activities fell within the framework and contributed to eventual attainment of the objectives.

The first requirement was that any activity be seminal; it had to either provide basic information necessary for future decisions, or had to have broad or long-range effects. The second requirement was, of course, that it must be affordable. Fortunately, the authorizing legislation for NCLIS did not strictly limit the Commission to its own appropriation. By enlisting direct and indirect support from other government agencies, from educational and professional institutions, from foundations, and from individuals, NCLIS was able to extend its activities beyond what could be funded from its own budget, and at the same time, obtained access to a larger body of expertise and involved a large community in its implementation efforts.

Let me explain the method of operation that was used by the Commission. With a small staff and a limited budget what was needed was staff ingenuity, strong commitment, and effort, and considerable restraint. The Commissioners were active in developing policy, determining implementation strategies, and suggesting research ideas. All task forces and project advisory committees included two or three Commissioners. Major contracts for research were usually co-sponsored and co-funded by another government agency, a professional society or a foundation. However, the most effective means of obtaining broadly based support for the Commission's efforts was the task force approach. A task force consisted of a group of experts and specialists assembled for a series of sessions to develop recommendations for solutions to a problem. Members were selected to represent a broad spectrum of interests and to provide the expertise necessary to a realistic solution. The number of participants varied from as few as ten to as many as twenty-five, depending upon the complexity and scope of the problem being addressed. The objective of each task force was clearly stated, a time frame and the number of meetings established, and a NCLIS staff member was assigned to provide coordination and support. In most cases two commissioners served as members of the task force.

I will not try to discuss in detail the many studies and activities undertaken by the Commission in the very active period of 1974-1980. You can read about them in the Commissioner's Annual Reports, in the many articles and comments published in the library press and, of course, the published results of the studies, reports and research. Instead, I will highlight some of the areas of controversy, impact, and influence.

The Commission in the early Seventies concentrated on the problem of the funding of public libraries and the limits of the funding partnership of the three levels of government. It advocated consideration of a realignment of the 83-12-5 local-state-federal percentages of funding, to a more equitable distribution, 50-30-20—the objective still far from being met. The impact has been to stir local and state librarians to work toward change. The greatest success has been at the state level. At the federal level the Commission suggested a reappraisal of the present categorical funding for libraries to a library and information block grant program. Fear and rivalry between school, public and academic libraries as well as the philosophy of the last two administrations has frustrated the effort. The Commission's efforts did serve as an impetus to the delegates to the White House Conference and resulted in two proposed national library and information science bills that emphasized greater cooperation and coordination between all types of libraries.

Copyright is an area where the Commission, under Dr. Frederick Burkhardt's leadership, and with the cooperation of Barbara Ringer, the Registrar of Copyrights, helped bring the library and publishing community together and kept them talking until a reasonable compromise was reached. The Commission sponsored and helped fund the first King Research, Inc. study of library photocopying which provides baseline data for activity before the 1976 copyright law. The Commission was also responsible for the five year review clause in the legislation contending that the rapid changes in technology required a review more frequently than the many decades that passed before the 1976 revision.

The close working relationship with the Library of Congress was reflected in the study which involved networking issues and national bibliographic control, the issue of the role of an authority file and the responsibility for providing that function in a network. The study recommendations were published in the report, "The Role of the Library of Congress in the Evolving National Network."

Who can forget the major effort over a four-year period to try to establish a National Periodical System. The result was Part D of Title II of the Higher Education Act. An opportunity that neither the library community nor the Commission was willing to utilize. The problem has not gone away. Some say the NPC was an idea whose time has passed. Others resignedly gave in to the private sector. Some of us feel frustrated and somewhat cynical. OCLC's ILL subsystem has helped but has not eliminated the need for a cost-effective service of a national periodical system.

The public/private sector issues were a concern of the Commission from 1975 and resulted in the establishment of a task force in 1978. Its report issued in early 1982 has stirred much discussion and controversy. This is an excellent example of another commission effort to directly confront a major issue, involve a broad constituency in its discussion, study and recommendations. The study certainly doesn't resolve the public/private sector problems, but it provides the ideas and suggestions that, if accepted, could well lead to a resolution and softening of many of the issues of controversy. Addressing each issue and working toward solutions requires commitment, patience and continuing effort. I am not optimistic.

The Commission recognized early the importance of library statistics and continuing education. One of its major efforts in the former was the inventory of the needs for library service. The study developed indicators of need and applied those to NCES statistical data on libraries. It clearly showed how grossly underfunded were libraries in 1971, how poorly staffed they were and how many gaps there were in their collections. The Commission's study on continuing education resulted in the establishment of a new national group—

CLENE—Continuing Library Education in Network Exchange. Its goal is to train trainers, to exchange information on continuing education, to assure quality in continuing education offerings.

The role of public and academic libraries in regional and national networking has always received attention and both types of institutions are involved in governance, funding and services. The Commission focused on the role of school and special libraries and established two task forces cooperating with both the American Association of School Librarians and the Special Library Association. The reports of these two task forces identify the services, offer concrete recommendations and identify implementation responsibilities.

In the area of technology, an NCLIS task force, working with the U.S. National Bureau of Standards and ALA's Library and Information Technology Association developed and prepared high level computer protocols that would permit the exchange of bibliographic information accessing different systems by the use of a standardized interface. Work toward defining, refining, and implementing these protocols has been under way by the LC and CLR these past five years.

The area of standards was addressed when an NCLIS task force, in 1977, assessed the functions of the American National Standards Institute Committee Z-39. It recommended the reorganization of governance, funding and operation. Implementation of the recommendation was started in 1978 and resulted in a restructuring—Z-39 is successfully operating today.

NCLIS started its active involvement in the international area in 1974 when Dr. Burkhardt addressed the IFLA opening session in New York. In 1977, the Commission took action and recommended to the President that he submit the protocol to the Florence agreement to the Senate for its ratification. NCLIS urged the Senate to take prompt and favorable action. IFLA in 1978 established an office on the Universal Availability of Publications (UAP). The Commission provided a two-year contract for some initial studies in Third World nations. Early in 1979, NCLIS was asked to consider supporting the U.S. participation in IFLA by assuming responsibility for one-half of the U.S. National dues with the other half coming from the various library and information associations. The recommendation was adopted.

In 1979 NCLIS established an International Cooperative Planning Group to study NCLIS's long term role in international activity.

Among the recommendations was one calling for the setting up of a task force but financial constraints made this impractical. It was agreed that the recommendations in the report would provide guidance to the Commission for possible future action in the international area.

Another important international responsibility that NCLIS was asked to assume was that of providing the secretariat services to support the U.S. National Committee for UNESCO General Information Program. This responsibility was also accepted by NCLIS effective in Fiscal Year 1983.

The Commission's concern for services to special constituencies was first addressed in a User's Needs Conference in 1972. The Conference report produced little new information or direction. The next area of concern was library services to the American Indian Community. A major effort was undertaken and culminated in the development of a long-range plan for Indian Library Services developed by the Bureau of Indian Affairs, the Department of Interior Library, and the Indian Community. The results of the effort is the recommendation for a new title in the proposed revision of the Library Sciences and Construction Act (LSCA).

Two other task forces set up in 1979 have just completed their reports and recommendations. These are the task force on Library and Information Services to Cultural Minorities and the Task Force on Community Information and Referral Services.

The White House Conference on Libraries and Information Services was the Commission's second opportunity (the National Program Document was the first) to identify needs, directions, and recommendations to the problems of providing effective library and information services to the residents of our nation. The effort to have such a conference authorized is well documented in the literature. The NCLIS staff's role in finally obtaining President Ford's agreement to request the funds from Congress, appoint the Advisory Committee and "call the conference" has never been appreciated or recognized except by the delegates to the national conference. In a very early speech I stated that even if the White House Conference was never held the preparatory conferences held in 49 states, the territories, and conferences for the American Indians and the Federal Librarians would produce a long range, lasting and positive impact on the awareness and improvement in library funding and services. I stand by that statement. The only concrete positive effects of the White House Library Conference recommendations have been at the state level. The Executive and Congressional branch of government since the fall of 1979 have never given more than lip service to the recommendations. The Commission, the national library associations, and the state library agencies have had little success on implementation of the recommendations. The major recommendation for a national library and information service act has been watered down into a proposed revision of the Library Science and Construction Act. Bold action and risk-taking is not one of the strengths of the three groups.

The White House Conference and the preparatory conferences were a success. They raised awareness; they created incentive and resulted in increased state level funding; they have provided a common bond between NCLIS, the national library and information science associations and the state library agencies. We may get some improvement in a revised LSCA, possibly a title for library services for the American Indians. We can do better.

From 1973 to 1979, NCLIS produced and published 25 studies and reports, 18 related papers and, of course, its annual reports. The preceding review referred to many of them. In that period the Commission produced its National Programs Document, planned, organized and ran the first White House Conference on Library and Information Services. Almost all of the accomplishments were under the leadership of Dr. Frederick Burkhardt, the Commission's distinguished scholar—Chairman. He understood the role of the Commissioners and the relationships of the staff. He made possible creative thinking and initiative. If NCLIS is to plan an important and influential role in the future, then the Dr. Burkhardt philosophy of leadership must be restored. The original reasons for establishing the Commission are as valid today as they were in the 60's. The law (PL 93-568) establishing the Commission clearly emphasized the role of libraries. In the Commission's first nine years its tilt was definitely toward libraries, library users, library services and public funding of such services. Since then its tilt has shifted toward the needs and interests of the private sector. NCLIS is in danger of losing its relevance in the eyes of the library community. What is needed is a balance. Both the library community and the private sector must work in a complementary fashion if the knowledge and information needs of society are to be met. The present commissioners and staff are certainly capable of meeting the challenge. But to

ALPHONSE F. TREZZA: "The White House Conference on Libraries and Information Services was the Commission's second opportunity (the National Program Document was the first) to identify library and information services to the residents of our nation. . . . The only concrete positive effects of the White House Library Conference recommendations have been at the state level."

do so will require a more aggressive stance, a greater concern for today's needs and services and less worry and concern of the future impact of technology. You can't solve tomorrow's problems if you don't fully understand and can cope with today's!

Let me close by stating that while I might not always agree with a specific action or direction, I strongly believe in and support the Commission—its members, its program, and its staff, especially its Executive Director. They are committed to fulfilling their legal mandate. But they cannot do it all alone. Nor will we always be in agreement, but we are all dedicated to the same goal.

We must be willing to support the Commission; to let them know how we feel about their activities, actions and national role. We must all become involved. No one agency, association or organization can solve all of the problems. We do need more national leadership, coordination and planning. But it will take all of us working together.

Successful planning to meet tomorrow's needs and to integrate the best of the developing technology for both service and administrative purposes has to be less "blue sky" and more realistic and achievable. The gap between technological change and advancement and acceptance by the average user is bigger than we would like to admit. It is fun to try to be a futurologist but it's more difficult and important to successfully meet the needs of our constituency today and in the near-term. Persistence and hard work and a commitment to our historic role of serving the needs and wants of our users as they define and demand them and not as we perceive them, must be our goal. Libraries will not become obsolete as a result of the technological revolution nor will they become irrelevant in spite of the dire predictions of the self-styled prophets of gloom and doom. Support and funding of libraries in the past five years has increased. I am optimistic about the future of public, school and academic libraries. Our greatest need in the next fifteen years is to have faith in ourselves, a commitment to our professional goals, a greater willingness to share resources without fear of diminishing services to our local users, a willingness to make certain that we are meeting our users' needs and desires rather than our professional perception of what they ought to have. Libraries have been, are, and will continue to be a basic public service, a public good. If you don't believe it you're in the wrong profession. Leave it and make room for those of us who are true believers.

ALPHONSE F. TREZZA: "In the Commission's first nine years its tilt was definitely toward libraries, library users, library services and public funding of such services. Since then its tilt has shifted toward the needs and interests of the private sector. NCLIS is in danger of losing its relevance in the eyes of the library community. What is needed is a balance. Both the library community and the private sector must work in a complementary fashion if the knowledge and information needs of society are to be met."

Panel Discussion

Lamont: At this point, we have, I think, three options. One of which I can ask all of my questions, but I'll defer. Secondly, you may ask your questions. If so, you must use your mike so that Wilson can get all of the comments into the proceedings. The third option is to let these five risk-takers go at each other and comment on each others' presentations. I'm going to choose—at least I'm going to try to be democratic, to begin with since they've all had a chance at dinner last night and so far today to open the comments up to all of you for any comments or questions. If not, the second option is going to be to let these five respond or react. Any questions or comments from the audience? Eva.

Question: Eva Brown, Chicago Library System. Al Trezza, you all referred to the National Periodical Center and the OCLC Interlibrary Loan subsystem. How about the OCLC union listing element in the series control subsystem? We have seen, I think, at least a beginning of the development of a national union list, in effect, of periodicals. Would you comment on that?

Trezza: Well, there are two problems. One is identifying where the information is, and that is admirably done in many ways. OCLC, of course, the Sears Control System, and many other ways are being on the union list of all kinds. But, in the final analysis it's delivery, it's document delivery, that counts. You see it's all well and fine to talk about the fact that in the year 2000 or 2010, or sometime like that, I can, at home, hit a button on my computer and look at all that business and get these printouts and all that is great. But the fact is that in the next ten years, it's not going to happen in a practical way. It may happen, experimentally in a limited way, but as far as in a broad way, it's not going to happen. If we had a center, we could produce the same day and put in the mail, or through electronic means, a particular item they needed because it would always be there. Now when the time comes as you can get the kinds of system that Dr. Kilgour is mentioning that they are working on right now with the content business in Dublin, you will have made the

ALPHONSE F. TREZZA: "You see it's all well and fine to talk about the fact that in the year 2000 or 2010, sometime like that, I can, at home, hit a button on my computer and look at all that business and get these printouts and all that is great. But the fact is that in the next ten years, it's not going to happen in a practical way. It may happen, experimentally in a limited way, but as far as in a broad way, it's not going to happen."

transition. But I contend that transition is nowhere near happening as people would like us to believe. I'll tell you why. They didn't move on implementation, of the title deed of the act. We fought very hard and we finally got the darn thing passed, but they put in two caveats which were very devastating and made everybody discouraged and made everyone throw up their hands and say, "The heck with it." One caveat was that they had to do one more study once this advisory committee, board, or commission was appointed; and the other one was that they wouldn't fund that title until (this is the Higher Education Act) until the part which is A, B, and C, had been funded at least in 19—I forget the year, say 80 level, we'll say—and that it was clear that they wouldn't be funding at that level for the next couple of years. These are the two caveats. So with that then, everyone took their hands and said the heck with it. Now, I tried to suggest there was a way towards moving towards implementation. You know, politics is the art of the possible, right? Fred pointed out how to get a lot of things regardless of problems because they were determined to do it and they overcame them. He heard the other networks the same way. We could have overcome that one too. How? Simple. If the Commission had really believed it, they would have gotten the President to appoint the advisory committee, which the law permitted. No money. OK, no money. We have the Committee. We think we could have gone to all these foundations who were bleeding about the National Periodical System and got them to give us some money to do two things: fund the meetings of this Committee and fund that study. Once that was finished, going back to Congress and getting the money would have been a lot easier, but nobody was willing to make the effort, or to fight. They just threw up their hands instead.

Lamont: Questions, comments from the audience? Please come up and use the mike.

Question: Dr. Kilgour, your presentation was extremely stimulating. I was intrigued by a novel idea, it is to me, about the OCLC content retrieval system. Could you kindly tell us something more about it, please?

Kilgour: [Content retrieval] into libraries but not into homes, and essentially it mimics the Xerox machine. But it has the potential of doing a great deal more and it will be doing more than just a simple delivery in paper form of an article. We do not anticipate doing delivery in paper form with the OCRS system. A good deal of our thinking has been based on the activity of medieval scriptoria, where you had up until the 12th century a publication in the form of a retail activity. You went to a scriptorian and you arranged to have a book written for you. I remember many years ago, I was doing an evaluation of the Short Surgery of Bruno of Longoburo [sic]—a manuscript that had been done in the 13th century from some surgeon, I don't know who it was. But when I got to the section—this was for a New York book dealer—(you know we in academe really earn our money by doing something besides collecting our pay checks, and that was one thing I used to do), but this manuscript, when I got to the section on dentistry it just wasn't there. The same was true when I got to the section on fractures, and it was quite clear that this surgeon wasn't going to fool around in people's faces and he wasn't going to try to set fractures, which was a miserable activity in the Middle Ages. So he didn't pay to have those parts of the book reproduced. If you look at the other area, let's say the Canterbury Tales, there are very few manuscript copies of all the Canterbury Tales. They're mostly just a single tale because somebody was interested in that, liked it, and didn't pay for having the whole thing reproduced the way you do now when you buy a copy of the Canterbury Tales. Although in the OCLC system since 1980 there has been one tale reprinted and there have been two selections, but neither one of those was done for me. So, we've had to look at the Middle Ages in designing this system. In the Middle Ages you didn't refer to page numbers, you referred to "near the beginning of the chapter four of the second book of Galen's *De Uso Medicorum*" or something like that, because page numbers were not significant. In a content retrieval system, the intelligent way to do it is to format the content for the device on which it's going to be displayed. These can be all different kinds of devices, which means you don't use the pages of the printed text, although we will be doing that at the very beginning, but we're designing it so that this will not be necessary to do. In Loughborough (in England) there is a professor, Brian Shackle, who has an extensive investigation on the electronic publishing of journals. He begins with the writing of an individual article on word processing and goes right through to the end user's use of the material. He has this system operating, at OCLC we are a participant in this system, but in order to be a participant, it really isn't OCLC, it's I. It's done on an individual basis. You have to submit for electronic publication a journal article, which I have done, and which will appear and be available only in electronic publication at least for a while, and never in paper form from Loughborough. How-

FREDERICK G. KILGOUR: "We do not anticipate doing delivery in paper form with the OCRS system. A good deal of our thinking has been based on the activity of medieval scriptoria, where you had up until the 12th century a publication in the form of a retail activity. You went to a scriptorian and you arranged to have a book written for you. . . .

In a content retrieval system, the intelligent way to do it is to format the content for the device on which it's going to be displayed. These can be all different kinds of devices, which means you don't use the pages of the printed text, although we will be doing that at the very beginning, but we're designing it so that this will not be necessary to do."

ever, you have these same problems and the way Brian Shackle has solved the page problem is that he numbers the paragraphs so that the references in the immediate future will be, both in journals and in books, I'm quite sure, to paragraph numbers. You could do it by line numbers but that doesn't make much sense because they wander around in size so that the numbers will change, but a paragraph number is permanent, so to speak. Now I'm going into this in some detail to let you know that there is a lot of work and a lot of imagination that has to go into this activity, just to get it started. Also, you are involved not just in the technique but also in the commercial aspects of it. I've talked with publishers about making texts available and spent some time just last week with the New England Journal of Medicine with respect to their making a text available to the other system that is going on at OCLC. When I talked with the publishers, I told them I don't want to get involved with copyright because, as far as I'm concerned, copyright is just another way of saying revenue and the important thing from their point of view is how do they get revenue out of the content retrieval system? They don't have any trouble with that kind of an approach, so that, really, OCLC will become a kind of book jobber supplying the catalog entry, the contents pages, index pages, and connections with the text wherever that may be—it might be at the publisher, it might be at OCLC. It will be transparent to the user and it doesn't make any difference where it will be; but from the viewpoints of economy of scale, it should be only in one place not occupying a huge amount of memory space. These relationships with the publishers will have to be worked out. They shouldn't be very difficult because they will be getting more money, they will not have huge amounts of paper on which nothing is printed and huge amounts of paper on which books are printed and bound that are in store bins. (They can have if they wish, now this won't be true in the early days, just one copy and that one copy will go back to the Middle Ages whereby, they are in both the wholesale and retail business with only one copy and this means a great difference to them in terms of revenue. It's going to increase it considerably.)

Several weeks ago a group of senior executives in the publishing business, mostly from the continent and under the leadership of the Director or President, I guess he is, of the International Electronic Publishing Research Center in Leatherheads in Surrey, England, of which I'm a Director—I mean, I'm on the Board of Directors—visited OCLC. The publishers were asking questions just the way librarians used to ask questions: How will we begin and what do we do? I've always thought this kind of a question is sort of like as though electronic publishing or on-line shared cataloging or microcomputers is an appliance like a vacuum cleaner or a television set, you just plug it in and it hums. It's not, it really isn't. It's very high technology and I can conclude by saying, as I concluded in talking with those publishers, that OCLC will do a great deal for them and we will. We have done a great deal for libraries and we're going to have to do a great deal for publishers, but the main purpose is getting information to the end users, and I'm sure, just as sure as I'm standing here, that we're going to make a contribution to publication just as we made a contribution to libraries. Is that enough? OK.

Question: Dr. Kilgour, I was wondering why it was so hard for foreign titles and publications to be on there for research. Do you have trouble finding the information that you need so that we can find it on OCLC?

Kilgour: I'm not quite sure I understood the question. Would you want to try it on me again?

Question: OK. I use OCLC on a regular basis and when researching to find more information on the piece I go to OCLC for that, but I find I have a lot of trouble finding foreign titles on OCLC, because of the simple fact that they're not there yet for some reason. I thought maybe you could tell me why?

Kilgour: I can give you—where do you get the references to search these titles?

Question: Well, in our office we have general formats that we use OCLC for.

Kilgour: No. How do you know. . .

Question: Oh, we use title pages and ISSN numbers and ISBN numbers.

Kilgour: Well, I would avoid using ISBN numbers for a whole variety of reasons, not the least of which is that many of them are wrong. I would also suggest that you use the minimum search key; in other words, when you're searching a title use the 3,1,1,1 key not the 3,2,2,1; or if you're using the author/title use the 3,3 not the 4,4 key. Quite often, and for reasons that are understandable, there are more mistakes made in references to foreign titles than there are—or I should say to non-English titles than to English titles; however, they certainly occur there. I'll give an example: I was once testing a random sample of requests to the British Library Lending Division that they had been unable to find anywhere, not just within BLLD but external to BLLD. They sent me one hundred—there were three duplicates, so there were actually ninety-seven—but in the references the French article "le" was "la." If you used "la" you wouldn't have gotten it, but when you used "l" you did get it even though the "a" was incorrect. It should have been "e." This is the kind of error that keeps occurring, particularly in non-English titles that you can find, so I would encourage you to do that. Incidentally, the way it came out was that 57% of the things that BLLD could not locate were in the OCLC data base. Of the 100%, 11% were bad titles, like the le/la thing I was telling you about. But, when they were corrected like, the . . . what was one . . . one was the *Basic Uses of Economic Information* or something like that. It was a totally different title, so that no matter how you searched you couldn't find it, but when you searched it under the author in OCLC you could find what the correct title was. Eleven percent were wrong, ghosts that got straightened out. So, by using the minimum keys, you can get. . . well, I got 57% instead of 46%, as I probably would have if I would have just done it using the major keys and nothing else. That's the only kind of help I can give you.

Lamont: Other questions from the audience? Do the panelists have anything they'd like to say at this point?

Kilgour: I have a question I want to ask Jim. This isn't some sort of a theoretical question without substance because I'm the Chairman of the Board and Acting President of a new major research center coming into being and there is a group of members or sponsors (or what you will) puzzling along as to how it might be organized from that point of view. You remember that Jim said each institution in AMIGOS had one vote and at times that caused problems. In the Ohio College Library Center it was set up the same way; in other words, the Riverside Methodist Hospital had one vote in the same way that the Ohio State University had a vote, although probably Ohio State must have paid a hundred times more than . . . but it's the way a legal cooperative is set up and in a legal cooperative no matter how many shares you own, everyone has got one vote. I'd just like to know a little bit about the problems you experienced here. If there are any elephant traps, I want to stay out of them.

Kennedy: Well, you hit the nail on the head. Basically, the larger libraries felt that they had contributed more in kind or in resources to the organization than the smaller libraries and yet, as it turned out, as the network kept growing in size and numbers of members

FREDERICK G. KILGOUR: "I have a question I want to ask Jim. . . . I'm the Chairman of the Board and Acting President of a new major research center coming into being and there is a group of members or sponsors (or what you will) puzzling along as to how it might be organized from that point of view. . . . Jim said each institution in AMIGOS had one vote and at times that caused problems. In the Ohio College Library Center it was set up the same way; . . . it's the way a legal cooperative is set up and in a legal cooperative no matter how many shares you own, everyone has got one vote. I'd just like to know a little bit about the problems you experienced here."

you had maybe twenty institutions that contributed more than 50% of the annual revenue for AMIGOS and the other two hundred plus institutions made up the rest. There was always a concern at membership meetings and voting that if we ever allowed the smaller libraries to caucus and get together that they could change the situations quite radically. That never happened although I'm sure that it crossed people's minds. Just like Mike was saying, when you're trying to work on fee schedules and so forth, you spend a lot of time on that also, and the concern there again is how do you, how could you, do this in a less democratic way? I mean the idea of one member one vote is a very democratic way, but in actuality it probably would make better sense to have voting shares based on contribution or size of library. Size of libraries, in this case, could be in a range; it wouldn't have to be as you add more volumes you now get another vote, etc., unless you went from one plateau to another. I just brought that up as a comment. I don't know that AMIGOS will ever change, and maybe the other networks will not either, but I know that in some other networks they are concerned the same way. The larger libraries tend to contribute more at the beginning of the organization like AMIGOS and maybe the one that you're beginning to direct is like that. You know it's small enough and everybody wants to help everybody else and they are not concerned about who is contributing more or less because they want to get it going, they want to make it successful. It's after a while that you start worrying about, "Hey, I contributed more," etc. and so forth. In other words, the marriage is dulling a little bit and so, therefore, not everybody is contributing 100%. You're looking to say, "Gee, I contributed more than so and so." So there's no easy answer at all, I'm afraid.

Bruer: There was a well-known founder of another cooperative in a foreign land who said, "From each according to his abilities and to each according to his needs."

Lamont: Alice, do you want to make a comment about that, about governance? No, no, OK. No, it wasn't directed to you.

Trezza: On governance, probably, let's assume there are three issues which I find are most difficult in all of this cooperation sharing of groups. One is governance, one is funding, and one is fear. I always put fear first, that's the biggest. Funding we can sometimes work out. Fear we can never get around. Governance we ought to be able to handle. The difficulty is you don't make the decision on governance later, you make it at the beginning when it's all theoret-

JAMES H. KENNEDY: "Basically, the larger libraries felt that they had contributed more in kind or in resources to the organization than the smaller libraries and yet, as it turned out, as the network kept growing in size and numbers of members you had maybe twenty institutions that contributed more than 50% of the annual revenue for AMIGOS and the other two hundred plus institutions made up the rest. . . . The larger libraries tend to contribute more at the beginning of the organization like AMIGOS and maybe the one that you're beginning to direct is like that."

ical and you haven't got any big controversies going. See, once the operation is going, it's much harder to get change. So it seems to me what you have to do is to think of proportional representation rather than direct representation. You have to . . . for example, when we were setting up the systems in Illinois it was very clear that the headquarters of the library which had the most books, the greatest amount of effort, had to have a permanent seat on the Board no matter what. The others could vote for representative people on the board, so you have to decide what you want and it's a lot easier to knock it out before you're organized than it is to change it later on, because once people get entrenched they won't give it up. At the beginning it's the initial agreement. You can fine tune it, but you can't really change it. And remember, the United States has two ways of doing it, right? We have the House of Representatives and the Senate, and that's a pretty good system. Sometime that's a model we ought to think about.

Bruer: I'm sort of under the opinion we've spent too much time wrestling with governance questions. I rather like the way . . . I referred earlier today to different types of libraries or segments as they are called in California. In my experience at CLASS, I came to a very high degree of appreciation for the special library community. To overstate it just a little bit, they don't really care about how things are organized; they want to accomplish things. They seize opportunities and they grab them and run with them and make something work for them, and they don't spend a whole lot of time bellyaching about whether a thing is put together in a representative fashion or not.

Lamont: I'd like to hear you all comment a little bit more on what I call the network personality. Jim talked about network directors as entrepreneurs and development of networks based on either the leadership at the top or the demands of the members. Alice talked about environment and personalities dictating network structure, and Michael talked about knowing the mission and determining that mission and taking a look at who was really involved in the network structure. I think all five of you are risk-takers and we talked a little bit at dinner last night about where the leaders in networking are, what's really going to happen now that networks have evolved. I'm wondering if you have any strong feelings about what kind of people should go into leadership and networking activities?

Bruer: I have a lot of strong feelings about a lot of things, but relevant to the issue you've raised, I can remember my early days,

ALPHONSE F. TREZZA: "On governance, probably, let's assume there are three issues which I find are most difficult in all of this cooperation sharing of groups. One is governance, one is funding, and one is fear. I always put fear first, that's the biggest. Funding we can sometimes work out. Fear we can never get around. Governance we ought to be able to handle."

J. MICHAEL BRUER: "I'm sort of under the opinion we've spent too much time wrestling with governance questions."

perhaps years, at CLASS and I would get occasionally passionate about an issue that I didn't think was getting through. The issue, as I saw it was, here was a regional network CLASS. It belongs to you, the owners of this network. You can make it do whatever you want to do with it. You merely have to step forward and seize it, but in fact that didn't actually happen. It doesn't happen often enough to suit me, not only in my own particular CLASS experience, but in other areas that I have had some association. So I don't know what kind of person it takes to be in the network. I alluded earlier to the fact it seems like it more and more takes a person who looks at things from a sort of commercial standpoint as opposed to what I would have thought a regional cooperative network would be about, and therefore, what kind of headset the people who manage the network ought to have. CLASS never did function as a coordinating organization for statewide planning, getting everybody together, "doing all types of library service to the user" sort of thing and the participating members never looked at CLASS that way themselves. They looked at CLASS as vendor. CLASS had to respond (because there was no other way to do it), it had to respond as a vendor. It has to respond as a vendor now. It's my contention that's very frequently, if not always, the case with networks; and because of that then it's another kind of person. When I came out of library school my idea was I'm going to be a librarian, I'm going to work in academic libraries and I'm eventually going to be the director of an academic library because I had ideas about professionalism and academics and all that sort of thing. There is nothing wrong with all that, but that kind of headset and related ones, public librarians and so forth, is not what goes down in making a network work.

Trezza: What Mike is trying to say is that he had become materialistic and crass and he wants money and not commitment. Sorry, Mike, I couldn't resist it. You know, the whole problem with leadership when you talk about leader organizations, you talk about national organizations such as OCLC or NCLIS, or state libraries. . . first of all, it's a matter of time. Sometimes you are in your right place at the right time to make an impact and you don't, or you do, as the case may be. Sometimes the right individual is there and the chemistry of that person on the people trying to organize an activity takes hold. It's hard to define exactly what it is. There are all kinds of articles on leadership. I just assigned two of my classes a few weeks ago to read a series of articles on leadership and to write their reactions to the whole issue. There must have been eight or nine ar-

J. MICHAEL BRUER: "CLASS never did function as a coordinating organization for statewide planning, getting everybody together, 'doing all types of library services to the user' sort of thing and the participating members never looked at CLASS that way themselves. They look at CLASS as a vendor."

ticles and every one, of course, had a different view on how you exert leadership. First of all it seems to me, from a personal view, you need someone who is willing to work very hard. You have to be committed to what you're doing, you really have to believe it; you have to be willing to take hard knocks, to take risks; you have to have imagination and creativity and you have to have a lot of gall; and you have to be a politician. You just have to fight every step of the way. You have to know when to push and when to pull. I used to call it the carrot and the stick. You know the old one of the carrot and the stick. Works beautifully—if you have the right mix. Too much carrot you're in trouble, and too much stick you're in trouble. The big trick is to keep the two going and keep your people off balance; don't give them a chance to breathe. They used to say to me, "Can't we rest?" I said, "Hell, no." Because once they rest you're in trouble. So what you do is you keep them going so much that they can't do anything but work. Then movement starts, and also almost anything is possible, if you really want it to happen. OCLC would never have happened without the kind of personal drive and commitment of Fred. It was just impossible. You could have put fifty people there and it would not have happened. It was the right mix at the right time. I'll use Dr. Burkhardt as my example for the Commission. He was the right person at the right time in that instance. This is true in all these organizations, so it's all well and fine to talk about how we're going to train them in library school, but believe me you cannot train people in library school to be entrepreneurs, to be business managers, catalogers, reference librarians, children's librarians, and everything else all in one year, or in two, or in five. The MBA's don't even succeed in doing this so why should we? So don't go telling me, Mike, about how we library schools ought to be training entrepreneurs. We might give them some of the highlights of it but we sure can't train them.

Bruer: I'm not quite yet prepared to say what library schools ought to be teaching. The nut of the issue I'm trying to raise is that the profession needs to look at the issue (as Bridget raised it) about what kind of people, from what kind of background, what kind of training appear to be needed on the network side. Do we want networks to operate that way, professionally speaking, or do we want them to operate in a kind of textbook theoretical way that at least I thought networks were going to operate when I got into it? But from my experience, it appears a lot of them don't operate that way, and I just want the question looked at objectively and openly and come to

ALPHONSE F. TREZZA: "You have to be committed to what you're doing, you really have to believe it; you have to be willing to take hard knocks, to take risks; you have to have imagination and creativity and you have to have a lot of gall; and you have to be a politician."

some decision on it. It may reflect back again on what we want to do in library schools, I don't know yet, but it's possible.

Kennedy: Let me try to answer it another way. I think that one thing that we've gladly stayed away from is the definition of a network. Of course, you have all types of organizations that might call them consortia, networks, or whatever. Depending on their function and their history and so forth, that will usually determine the type of person, the type of background that is required. Just for example, just because AMIGOS did what it did for eight years doesn't mean that, prior to the selection of my successor they decided that, "maybe we'll want to change directions now that we have JK out of the way" or, "he's left and therefore we are looking for another type of person." I think you've seen that in some of the other network organizations. So I don't think there is any one thing, except that if the organization is in fact out there to deliver products, new services, and so forth you would need somebody that has some sort of marketing skills, some way of demonstrating or convincing people that this is the best thing and they should take it on and so forth and so on, or at least convince them that that somehow we've got a printing press for money in the basement and therefore it's not going to cost them anything for development. But, there's no easy answer. I had a motto on the wall of my office that said, "I can't tell you what the secret of success is, but the secret of failure is trying to please everyone." I never did.

Wilcox: It may be that it's the definition of a network that determines what the leadership of networks should be, but I would suggest it should be a question of what kind of a network. If the networks are going to be cooperatives, then I would suggest that you need the kind of a person who can create an environment that's conducive to cooperative and collaborative work, and that means that the librarians are going to be doing the work. If you're interested in creating a network that's a business, then you'll want to have somebody who is going to be able to buy and sell and deal in a legal fashion with contracts and other ways. I think the kind of person that's going to be involved is probably more determined, or will be determined, by the kind of networks we have.

But in any event, what you want is somebody who is successful, and if they aren't successful then you want some way to get rid of them. A friend of mine once said, "Maybe what we were doing was stumbling blindly on the cutting edge of mediocrity."

Lamont: We're going to have a little bit more discussion but,

J. MICHAEL BRUER: "The nut of the issue I'm trying to raise is that the profession needs to look at the issue (as Bridget raised it) about what kind of people, from what kind of background, what kind of training appear to be needed on the network side. Do we want networks to operate that way, professionally speaking, or do we want them to operate in a kind of textbook theoretical way that at least I thought networks were going to operate when I got into it? But from my experience, it appears a lot of them don't operate that way . . . ''

JAMES H. KENNEDY: "... you have all types of organizations that might call them consortia, networks, or whatever. Depending on their function and their history and so forth, that will usually determine the type of person, the type of background that is required...."

* * *

"I had a motto on the wall of my office that said, 'I can't tell you what the secret of success is, but the secret of failure is trying to please everyone.' I never did."

there is hot coffee and tea and you're welcome to get a cup for yourself whenever. According to my notes, Michael said that he thought library networks were becoming more competitive and actually starting to compete for members. He suggested that networks can function only on a competitive basis. I'm wondering if anyone would like to respond to that, agree, disagree, speak from their own experience. No, no, yes, OK, fine.

Kennedy: Mike, I had this question already and I'll phrase back. You said (or implied) that there could have been some better cooperation between networks and instead they're out competing with similar products, etc. Can you give some examples of where network cooperation could have taken place and, if so, do you know how this could have happened? There's no real group of network directors, per se, that can all agree on anything or agree to deliver product A or product B.

Bruer: That's quite true, there is no such group. There used to be, but it never did anything, and maybe the reason it didn't is because of what I was implying, or boldly stating. The networks—many networks, I never say never and I never say all—many networks could not perhaps function in that kind of collaborative environment even if that organization, which consisted of network directors, had succeeded in living and growing because of at least a couple of things. As Freddie said, the networks (many of the networks) are seen by their own constituent members as just another vendor. So it's not surprising that that kind of vendor attitude would exist at the top of the network, vis-a-vis, other networks. I said it may be that it is only in a competitive environment in which the regional and national networks can operate. I'm willing to accept that if it is reality, but I just don't want these sorts of things to happen more or less unconsciously, willy/nilly and we wake up ten years from now and we find that's the way things are. Let's say that that's the way they are now and say we like it that way.

Trezza: Many years ago, it seems like many years ago in the '70's, about '72 or '73, somewhere along in there, at the Commission we were having a discussion about national networking, who was going to do what. I had the temerity to suggest at that stage that what we might do is declare that we were going to throw our lot in with OCLC, in effect, endorse it as the arm of the national network. I was told, "No, we're a puristic society." RLIN (which didn't exist) was then BALLOT. Essentially, it was single institutions, one of them had some cooperation with other institutions. They all kept

ALICE E. WILCOX: "If the networks are going to be cooperatives, then I would suggest that you need the kind of a person who can create an environment that's conducive to cooperative and collaborative work, and that means that the librarians are going to be doing the work."

JAMES H. KENNEDY: "Mike, I had this question already and I'll phrase back. . . . Can you give some examples of where network cooperation could have taken place and, if so, do you know how this could have happened?"

J. MICHAEL BRUER: "... it may be that it is only in a competitive environment in which the regional and national networks can operate."

saying, "No, we have to wait; let the University of Chicago develop its system, let BALLOT develop a little further, the competition will be good, OCLC will be better for the competition." "Hindsight is great," I said, "before 20/20." It seems to me that an opportunity had passed. You look now, today, maybe we might not have had to have three or two or whatever national networks. Maybe we could have made a formation at that time. That's my example, when sometimes there's an occasion and a time when action might do something. You wait a year or two, three years later, it's past and you can't go back. That was an example. I was speaking out in the west some years ago and said that there are too many organizations out there. There were too many of these "darn networks," we ought to eliminate them all, or some of them, and mainly mention a couple. I'm pleased to say there was a period of a few years about three of them were born. There were just too many. Everybody wanted one just to have one. Right here in the midwest they wanted to form one. You want to know why when I asked them, "Why?" Because "everybody else had one, NELINET had one, SOLINET had one, AMIGOS had one, what about us in the midwest," you see? I said, "That's stupid, that's not a good enough reason. Why do you want it? Give me some concrete reasons." They went ahead and formed it. It didn't last. It died, because they never had an honest to goodness mission. It wasn't competition. It was lack of goals, lack of purpose, lack of opportunity. So it seems to me that if you're going to have these networks compete, they're fine as long as the competition is going to lead to improvement. But the people are thinking of competing to deny someone else the opportunity of becoming "the one." I think this is unfortunate and that's been part of the history in library networking.

Bruer: Lest there be any misunderstanding I just want to make it clear that I, myself, am not in favor of creeping monopolism.

Lamont: Any other questions or comments from the audience? Yes?

Question: I am Inja Hong from Hutchinson College, Kansas. I would like to address my question to Dr. Kilgour. How many terminals are connected to the OCLC at the moment and what is the total number that can be connected and searched simultaneously? I was always curious about that because of that large number we have seen.

Kilgour: Well, I don't know the exact figure at the present time but it's somewhere in the excess of 5,500 that are on the dedicated

ALPHONSE F. TREZZA: "... at the Commission we were having a discussion about national networking, who was going to do what. I had the temerity to suggest at that stage that what we might do is declare that we were going to throw our lot in with OCLC, in effect, endorse it as the arm of the national network. I was told, 'No, we're a puristic society.' ... They all kept saying, 'No, we have to wait; let the University of Chicago develop its system, let BALLOT develop a little further, the competition will be good, OCLC will be better for the competition.' 'Hindsight is great,' I said, 'before 20/20.' It seems to me that an opportunity had passed."

private telephone circuitry which now exceeds 180 thousand miles. There really isn't any technical limitation. This excludes, by the way, the dial up terminals; those that are coming in over TYMNET and TELENET and direct dial up. I don't know how many they are but the institutions are somewhere in the number of eight hundred that participate that way and the participation is very small. It's only about 2% of the activity on OCLC. There really isn't any technical limitation to doing this. There are desirable changes in design, I think, for the use of the telecommunication system and there is some limitations. In the present kind of system, we can't use satellite communication because it is too slow, and therefore, too expensive for the participating libraries. But it can be expanded and expanded and expanded. I would guess that the real technical limitation is the number of users, potential users.

Lamont: Are there any other comments from the audience, last comments from the panelists? The panelists are supposed to be getting us towards the year 2000, so this is your chance. Jim?

Kennedy: Al, I'm sorry. As I told you last night you had to speak a little slower, so I know that you touched on this subject but from your perspective now, what should the Commission be doing and/or why? Why is it really necessary now as opposed to when you were there?

Trezza: I recently read an article by Henrietta Avrum who many of you know from the Library of Congress. She is commenting about the various problems with the group she works with. She has a group called The Network Advisory Committee which is made up of representatives of all the various networks. They meet a couple of times a year and discuss common issues. She said in one of these talks, "There is still the lack of national coordination and national leadership and we still need it in Washington." The National Commission was supposed to provide that national leadership and that national coordination. That's why it was not an operating body. It was not supposed to be threatening, you see. It was supposed to provide this leadership and that's what they attempted to do. What's happened is that when it looked like it might succeed, all of a sudden fear rose. So everybody then wanted to kind of to dampen it some and the private sector got very excited and started indicating that the librarians were trying to take over the world and that we were forgetting about the private sector and how they really make information happen and how we are only the ones that we're sort of the funnel in which it goes through, that they provide it, they are the

J. MICHAEL BRUER: "Lest there be any misunderstanding I just want to make it clear that I, myself, am not in favor of creeping monopolism."

FREDERICK G. KILGOUR: "Well, I don't know the exact figure [of terminals connected] at the present time but it's somewhere in the excess of 5,500 that are on the dedicated private telephone circuitry which now exceeds 180 thousand miles. There really isn't any technical limitation. . . . There are desirable changes in design, I think, for the use of the telecommunication system and there is some limitations."

entrepreneurs, the creativity people, and all this business. So what happened then, the Commission started looking away from some of these ideas. They kind of moved back. I do think the Commission is important. I do think it needs to continue, but I do think it needs to go back on track, going back on track is the thing. They have to worry less about the complaints of a few and more about the main road. The main road by the law is what it says, how you provide information to people. How do you and I as individual users, individuals, get what we want when we want it in a timely fashion and a way we can afford it. We only get it on making sure it's available through this tremendous network of libraries all over the country: academic, school, public and special. There's nothing that is going to replace that network. You can improve it, you can enhance it, you can use technology as an instrument of it, but you're not going to replace it. The library as an institution is not going to be overtaken by individual entrepreneurs or the information specialists who go out and set up their own little thing and provide special services. But where do they get their information? From the library. You close your doors, they couldn't operate. You bet the Commission is necessary, but it's not going to work if you and I don't do something about it. For example, I read you there are fourteen members in the Library of Congress. If you had looked at it, it's hard to listen to this, it says there that there has to be five people on it representing the libraries. Look at the list sometime of the current Commissioners. You'll find three. One is the Librarian of Congress, of the three. The Chair who is a librarian; Julia Wu, school librarian; and the Librarian of Congress. All the others are either trustees (library trustees), or business people, or information specialists. Well, you and I shouldn't stand for it. We should be screaming to our Congressmen saying, "That's against the law!" Say to the Reagan administration, "No, you must appoint librarians! Don't reappoint the same old people all the time." So, the Commission can't do its job if you and I don't let it. Now the other answer is to let it die and the Reagan administration tried to do that. They tried to zero fund it. So did the Carter administration, by the way. It might come as a surprise to many of you but just before the White House Conference, they tried to zero fund it. Well obviously it put them in an embarrassing position so they backed off. How do they explain to one of those conferences that they zero funded the Commission, you see? So they backed off. But the Reagan administration promptly went and tried to zero fund it. Congress wouldn't permit it to happen. I don't

ALPHONSE F. TREZZA: "She [Henrietta Avrum] has a group called The Network Advisory Committee which is made up of representatives of all the various networks. They meet a couple of times a year and discuss common issues. She said in one of these talks, 'There is still the lack of national coordination and national leadership and we still need it in Washington.' The National Commission was supposed to provide that national leadership and that national coordination. That's why it was not an operating body. It was not supposed to be threatening, you see."

think Congress or the library profession would permit the Commission to be zero funded. But I don't think it should operate if it doesn't do our bidding because that's why it was established. I keep going back and reading the law over and over again, and before I wrote this talk I read it again to say, "Do I still think it's valid?" You bet! We need it, we need it badly. It hasn't quite done its job just right. What we have to try and do is to make sure that it does its job.

Kilgour: I'm going to repeat something that I published a while ago in a paper entitled "Public Policy and National and International Networks." It's my view that it's impossible to have a library or information policy in the United States and the reason for that is that the United States government is essentially a medieval government. In fact, it's the only still existing medieval government in the world. The Presidency of the United States is the only remaining constitutional medieval monarchy still in existence. What happened was that in the early 17th century the Tudor government, which was a medieval government, was transplanted to North America. It was brought here because it was in trouble in the United Kingdom, there was Oliver Cromwell and others who were raising a fuss and many came here to avoid it and brought their medieval government. We still have it. It's all checks and balances. It's like the Magna Carta which was a design to keep King John from imposing on the nobles. We've got fifty nobles, fifty fiefdoms in the form of State Governors and below them they're got a lot of fiefdoms either with whom they have to compete. You can't go to one place in the United States government and you don't have a rationalization of authority the way you do in modern governments. When Mrs. Thatcher goes somewhere and says so and so it sticks. But when the President of the United States, no matter who, it doesn't depend who the individual is, goes somewhere the classic case is Wilson in the League of Nations that didn't stick although it was his idea. There are three places in the United States government that are responsible for running the United States, so to speak. There's the Congress, the Presidency, and the Supreme Court that can tell either one of them that they are wrong, and as far as the President is concerned make it stick (and the Congress usually sticks with the Congress although they can make changes). So given this situation recently for example, the British Library proposed to have a UKLDS. I've forgotten exactly what it stood for, but it was a central data bank of machine readable cataloging records that would be available to British libraries and to

ALPHONSE F. TREZZA: "We should be screaming to our Congressmen saying, 'That's against the law!' Say to the Reagan administration, 'No, you must appoint librarians! Don't reappoint the same old people all the time.' So, the Commission can't do its job if you and I don't let it."

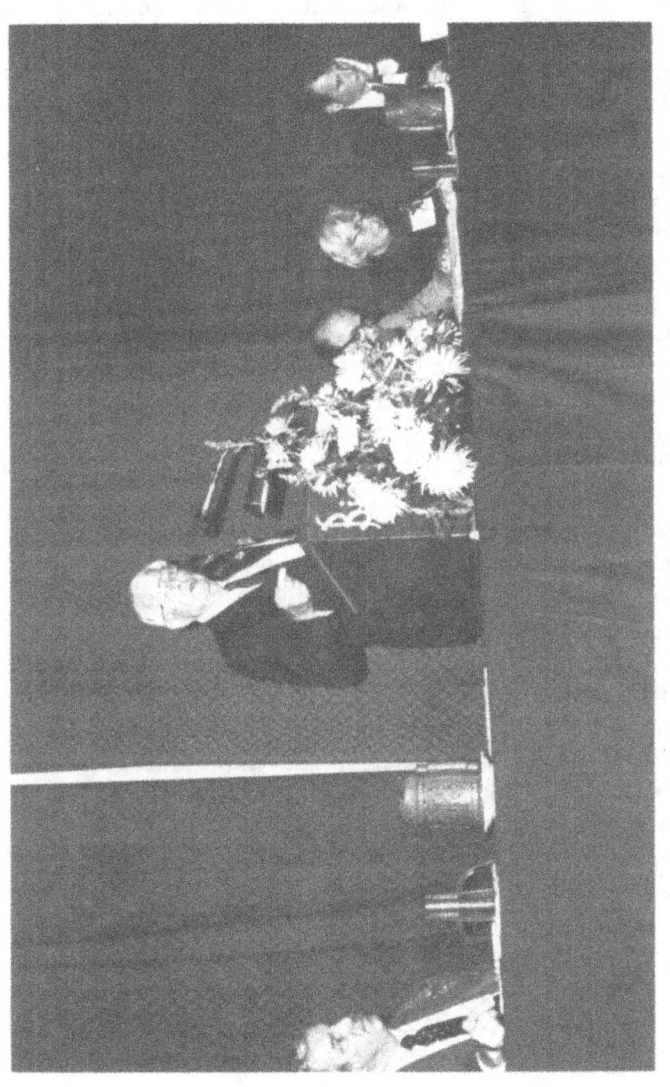

FREDERICK G. KILGOUR: "It's my view that it's impossible to have a library or information policy in the United States and the reason for that is that the United States government is essentially a medieval government. In fact, it's the only still existing medieval government in the world."

* * *

"I'll make one other statement, and that is, if it were possible to have a national policy and if we had had one, there wouldn't have been an OCLC. There would have been something very different that would have been essentially a government agency."

the small cooperatives that are in the United Kingdom. That no longer is a possibility because they went to the Ministry of Culture to request the funds to support it, and The Ministry of Culture said, "No thank you!" There isn't any other place in the United Kingdom to go and get the funds. This is not true, as you know, in the United States. You can go here, there, and almost everywhere and drum up some kind of support. But given that situation where would you have a national policy established? The National Commission can't do it. It can participate in it. The Presidency can't do it. The Supreme Court certainly can't do it. It's conceivable that the Congress could do it, but how would it do it? It doesn't do that kind of thing. So I don't think you can look forward to having a national policy established here in the United States. I'm not sure, given our type of government that it's even desirable to try to do it. Certainly, in the modern governments of Europe, and that's just as true of east as well as western Europe, you can do this kind of thing. You can then operate it, you have central control of the funds that fund the public libraries, that fund the academic libraries. These things don't exist in the U.S. We do it a different way. I'll make one other statement, and that is, if it were possible to have a national policy and if we had had one, there wouldn't have been an OCLC. There would have been something very different that would have been essentially a government agency. Now that may look bad to you from your experience with American government, but with modern governments where authority is rationalized it wouldn't have been bad.

Lamont: Michael Bruer, Alice Wilcox, Al Trezza, Fred Kilgour, and Jim Kennedy—thank you for sharing your experiences and your philosophies with us. Thank you for coming to Illinois. We've appreciated your time.

Thank you.

LEFT TO RIGHT: Frederick G. Kilgour, J. Michael Bruer, Alice E. Wilcox, James H. Kennedy, Alphonse F. Trezza, Bridget L. Lamont, and The Honorable Wayne Anderson.

For Product Safety Concerns and Information please contact our EU
representative GPSR@taylorandfrancis.com
Taylor & Francis Verlag GmbH, Kaufingerstraße 24, 80331 München, Germany

www.ingramcontent.com/pod-product-compliance
Lightning Source LLC
Chambersburg PA
CBHW052131300426
44116CB00010B/1856